AMERICAN
HEROES:

IN AND OUT OF SCHOOL

AMERICAN HEROES:
IN AND OUT OF SCHOOL

NAT HENTOFF

DELACORTE PRESS/NEW YORK

Published by
Delacorte Press
1 Dag Hammarskjold Plaza
New York, New York   10017

Manufactured in the United States of America

First printing

Library of Congress Cataloging in Publication Data
Hentoff, Nat.
American heroes.
Bibliography: p.
Summary: Focuses on the legal battles of ten students,
librarians, and others seeking to protect the Bill of
Rights, with an emphasis on the areas of free speech and
civil rights.
1. Students—Legal status, laws, etc.—United States—
Juvenile literature. 2. Civil rights—United States—
Juvenile literature. 3. Freedom of speech—United States
—Juvenile literature. [1. Freedom of speech. 2. Civil
rights. 3. United States—Constitutional law—Amendments
—1st–10th] I. Title.
KF4150.Z9H46 1987   342.73'085   86-29140
ISBN 0-385-29565-0   347.30285

For Rose Reissman, teacher,
Ditmas Junior High School, Brooklyn, New York.
Every year she makes the Bill of Rights
jump right off the page
into the lives of her students.

CONTENTS

School officials do not possess absolute authority over their students. Students in school as well as out of school are "persons" under the Constitution. They are possessed of fundamental rights which the State must respect, just as they themselves must respect their obligations to the State.

—United States Supreme Court, *Tinker* versus *Des Moines Independent School District,* 1969

INTRODUCTION

One day in Montello, a town of twelve hundred people in Wisconsin, the libraries in the high schools and the elementary school were raided. Not by the police, but by a group called Concerned Citizens. These members of the community believed that certain books were dangerous to young readers, so they took those books out of the libraries. Among them were J. D. Salinger's *Catcher in the Rye,* James Baldwin's *Nobody Knows My Name,* Paul Goodman's *Growing Up Absurd,* and Judy Blume's *Are You There God? It's Me, Margaret.,* and *Starring Sally J. Freedman as Herself.*

A number of teachers, librarians, and students were frightened by what had happened. It was as if Montello had become the scene for the movie version of Ray Bradbury's *Fahrenheit 451.* Would there be bonfires of banned books after the next raid? There was a town election coming up, and some of the librarians and teachers organized to help those candidates running for the board of education who pledged that they would not permit any more censorship of books in school libraries.

After the results were in, a majority of the new board of education did indeed agree that in a world where most people are told what to think, the very best way to learn to be free is to be free to learn.

I got to know Mary Maasz, one of the teachers in Montello who fought for free speech and the freedom to read. When the raid took place, she had said, "What has been happening here is frightening for anybody who cares about students. And the censoring of these books is personal, very personal, to anybody who believes that the First Amendment exists."

Mary Maasz and I corresponded as the free-speech fight in Montello went on, and I met her when I was in Wisconsin to give a talk about censorship. Knowing that she exists, that she takes the freedom-of-speech guarantee of the First Amendment so personally, makes me feel more confident that this is not a country that will let its heritage of free speech be taken away.

Oh, there'll be setbacks, and a lot of battles with the thought police. But as I've discovered all over the country, there are a good many First Amendment patriots, sons and daughters of Thomas Jefferson and James Madison, in our schools and libraries, as well as elsewhere in the community. There are also a lot of would-be censors, all right, but there still are people who believe with the late Supreme Court justice William O. Douglas that "restriction of free thought and free speech is the most dangerous of all subversions. It is the one un-American act that could most easily defeat us."

This book is about Americans, in and out of school, who keep fighting to protect the Bill of Rights—ranging from freedom of speech, press, and religion to everyone's right to privacy—so that the Bill of Rights can keep on protecting all of us.

Some of these real-life heroes are students, some are librarians and teachers, and there is that nonviolent battler for human rights everywhere, Joan Baez. There is also Adah Maurer, whose name may be new to you but who has done more than any other person in the history of this country to stop the official beating of children in the public schools.

This is a book about Americanism, about taking pride in belonging to the freest nation on earth—indeed, the freest in the history of the world. And so long as the young in this land know what their rights and liberties are—and are willing to work to preserve them—America will continue to be the freest nation on earth.

But if we ever have a generation that does not take the Bill of Rights *personally*, that does not understand or care about individual liberties, then our freedoms may become just a memory.

I

YOUNG PEOPLE WITH THE COURAGE OF THEIR CONVICTIONS

1

*The student who turned out
not to be a jerk at all.*

The town of Brunswick in south coastal Maine went through a bruising free-speech fight in 1984. At its center was seventeen-year-old Joellen Stanton, a senior at Brunswick High School. Until that year, she had never been controversial in school or in the town, but all of a sudden she somehow got the idea into her head that the First Amendment is real—something meant for personal use, not just words under glass.

Brunswick High School, like high schools across the nation, publishes a yearbook, and each departing senior gets to choose a brief quotation to accompany his or her picture. Some students choose inspirational quotes from presidents (Woodrow Wilson and John F. Kennedy). Most, however, have celebrated the pursuit of pleasure: "In heaven there is no beer, so we'd better drink it here." And: "Life is a waste of time, time is a waste of life. So let's get wasted and have the time of our lives."

But as for Joellen Stanton, she had been thinking about capital punishment, off and on, since she'd read Truman Capote's *In Cold Blood* in her sophomore year. At home she had talked about people on death row, particularly about whether people who commit such horrifying crimes should be killed by the state. Does the state then become a murderer too?

So for her yearbook quote she picked this excerpt from a January 24, 1983 *Time* magazine story on capital punishment:

The executioner will pull this lever four times. Each time 2,000 volts will course through your body, making your eyeballs first bulge, then burst, and then broiling your brains. . . .

Not a particularly cheerful farewell to Brunswick High, but Joellen Stanton said she wanted to try to "provoke some of my classmates to think a little more deeply than if I had written a standard butterfly quote."

The students in charge of the yearbook, the faculty advisers at the school, and the high school administrators were shocked and appalled at what Joellen Stanton had done. Her quote was, they said, "inappropriate," "in bad taste," "too graphic," and "unacceptable for public consumption."

The outraged principal, Gerald Millett, proclaimed that if this description of capital punishment were printed in the yearbook, it would be "disruptive to the community."

Joellen Stanton nonetheless refused to censor herself. With the help of the Maine Civil Liberties Union, she went to court, claiming that the First Amendment to the Constitution guaranteed her the right to free speech in her high school yearbook. And Federal District judge Gene Carter ruled that Brunswick High could not print the yearbook until this young woman's First Amendment rights were taken into account.

The judge quoted from an earlier decision by the United States Supreme Court: "The vigilant protection of constitutional freedoms is nowhere more vital than in the community of American schools." Joellen Stanton had something she wanted to say, and in this free country, she ought to be able to say it.

The judge also referred to a warning a classmate of Joellen had directed at her. If Joellen persisted in her stubbornness, said the classmate, a lot of the kids would consider her to be a "jerk" for insisting on that quote about capital punishment in the yearbook.

Well, said Judge Carter, in a free country everybody has a right to look like a jerk—if that's what people think of you after you speak your mind. "The First Amendment," he went on, "declares that the highest interest of the people is best served if government [in this case, the high school principal] is required to stay its hand and permit Joellen Stanton, and millions like her, to take upon their personal risk the ability of their ideas . . . to survive and propagate." The government has no right to prevent her from being a "jerk" by suppressing her ideas.

Taking risks is the very definition of being free. That's how America became free.

Joellen Stanton finally won because the school board, as the deadline for printing the yearbooks got very close, agreed to a settlement of the dispute. Her quotation would be printed, word for word, alongside her picture in the yearbook. Joellen, on the other hand, had to add a line: "This quote focuses on the reality of violence in today's society." By insisting on that line, the school board thought—incorrectly—that it had saved face, simply by insisting on a line of its own under Joellen's picture.

Actually, the "settlement" was a total victory for Joellen, who turned out to be a steadfast defender of the First Amendment and not a jerk at all. The other kids at Brunswick High had thereby learned what James Madison, the principal architect of the First Amendment, had wanted them to learn: a lone voice can successfully stand up against the great pressure of the majority, including the authorities.

2

*"Because Hitler didn't finish
the job right, we're going to."*

In September, 1984, the opening day of school at Randolph High School began, as do all days in that Massachusetts school, with the playing of "The Star Spangled Banner" on the public address system. As always, in every classroom students and teachers stood up for the national anthem and the pledge of allegiance to the flag.

One student, however, did not stand—Susan Shapiro, seventeen, and a senior. Her homeroom teacher, Mrs. Jean Noblin, ordered Susan to get up. Susan did slowly get up, but she had not given up. (And by persevering in fighting for her principles, Susan would wind up being scorned by most of the students in her school, while also being threatened by many adults across the country.)

The next school day, Susan showed Mrs. Noblin a pamphlet she had been reading at home. Published by the United States Government, it was titled *Your Legal Rights and Responsibilities: For Public School Students.* Susan Shapiro pointed to a line in the pamphlet:

"You may not be forced to take part in the salute to the Flag or Pledge of Allegiance if doing so violates your beliefs or values."

That decision had not been made by the writer of the pamphlet but rather by the United States Supreme Court in a 1943 case, *West Virginia State Board of Education* v. *Barnette*. The case had been brought all the way to the Supreme Court because a number of children of Jehovah's Witnesses had been expelled from school for refusing to salute the flag. The Jehovah's Witnesses believe that the Old Testament's prohibition against bowing to any "image" includes the flag.

In declaring that those children had the right to refuse to salute the flag, Justice Robert Jackson, speaking for a majority of the Court, pointed out that since this really is a free country, its people are free to differ. And that freedom to disagree "is not limited to things that do not matter much. That would be a mere shadow of freedom." In a truly free country, each of us has "the right to differ as to things that touch the heart of the existing order."

It is especially important, said Justice Jackson, that students in our schools learn that they have a right to differ. Jackson explained: "The fact that boards of education are educating the young for citizenship is reason for scrupulous protection of constitutional freedoms of the individual, if we are not to strangle the free mind at its source and teach youth to discount principles of our government as mere platitudes."

What's the point of reading about the Bill of Rights and other American freedoms in schoolbooks if they are not permitted to come alive in schoolrooms?

As for Susan Shapiro, her decision not to stand for the national anthem and the pledge of allegiance to the flag was not based—as it had been with the children of the Jehovah's Witnesses—on religious beliefs. But the courts, in a number of decisions after 1943, had made clear that a dissenter need not be religious to have the right to refuse to take part in these patriotic ceremonies. The state cannot compel anyone, irreligious or religious, to go against his or her conscience.

Susan Shapiro's conscience told her, as she said to me, that it made no sense to stand up and pledge allegiance to a symbol, a piece of cloth. "Boys go to war," Susan noted, "to protect the people, not the flag. It's the people who mean everything."

She was not trying to convert the other students to her beliefs. Susan simply did not want her own beliefs violated by being forced to stand. After all, in her junior year she had stayed seated all year while "The Star Spangled Banner" played and other students pledged allegiance to the flag. Her teacher then, Thomas Turner, himself stood and pledged allegiance, but he did not believe he had the right to force any of his students to do the same.

But Susan Shapiro's homeroom teacher in her senior year, Jean Noblin, did not agree with Thomas Turner. Mrs. Noblin told Susan Shapiro that her father had been a career army officer, that she had had students who had died for the flag, and it bothered her that this seventeen-year-old girl wouldn't stand up for the flag.

In reply, Susan said that the flag was only a symbol, a piece of cloth.

According to Mrs. Noblin, she answered Susan by saying, "Yes, it's a symbol, but so is the Cross and so is the Star of David." Then, Mrs. Noblin recalled, "I asked Susan how she would feel if someone spit on the Star of David."

Susan Shapiro was disturbed that Mrs. Noblin had made reference to her religion, but the teacher said no slur was intended. Susan thought otherwise.

The student was informed by school authorities that they recognized the Supreme Court's ruling in this matter and they would obey the law of the land. Susan could remain seated.

That would have been the end of the story except for the fact that the press picked it up—first local papers and television and eventually the wire services, *The New York Times*, and the *CBS Evening News With Dan Rather*.

As the publicity became more and more intense, practically all the teachers and all the students in the school rallied around Mrs. Noblin. Some of the kids even brought little

American flags to class to show which side *they* were on. And a reporter for the school newspaper told the Quincy *Patriot Ledger* that when students in his politics class discussed the case, many of them "were extremely angry and intolerant of Susan Shapiro. . . . It's hate and you could feel the hate."

One Randolph High School student told *CBS Evening News*, "She should have stood up. Everybody else does." Said another student, "She's going to an American high school in America, she should at least have the respect to stand up."

The rejection of Susan's right of conscience by her fellow students indicates that their teachers had failed to tell them about the First Amendment right of dissent as illuminated by court decisions in cases like hers. In a way, the students were acting out Justice Robert Jackson's warning:

"Compulsory unification of opinion achieves only the unanimity of the graveyard." As in Communist countries where the government decides what everyone shall think—and shall not think.

Or, as Gerald Rumbos, commander of the Veterans of Foreign Wars chapter in Randolph said publicly, "You can do anything you want in this country, but if you don't stand up for the flag, you don't belong in this country."

Sounding an eerie note, a group of students, hiding in the bushes behind the Shapiros' home, mockingly serenaded the family one Saturday night with "The Star Spangled Banner."

In school Susan was threatened with being beaten up, while other threats, invariably anti-Semitic, came to her home by phone and letter. "Because Hitler didn't finish the job right," said one caller, "we're going to." And one of many others added, "It *can* happen here! Think about it—*Jew!*"

To ensure her security in school, the Community Relations Division of the Justice Department in Washington arranged for escorts for Susan between classes. And the attorney general of Massachusetts tried to track down the death threats Susan and her family were getting at home.

Most of the kids at Randolph High School were not speaking to Susan. Before the academic year was over, Susan had enough credits to graduate; she could have avoided the cold silence, the stares, the snickers, and the threats by not attending classes anymore.

Susan would not retreat. "I'm going to keep going to school," she said. "I want to show them they can't push me around, that I'm not afraid of them."

There was a pause. "I love America," said Susan, who told me she would have voted for Ronald Reagan in 1984 had she been old enough. "Does anybody know that?"

On the Fourth of July, 1985, after Susan had graduated from Randolph High School, a small bomb exploded on the lawn outside Susan Shapiro's home. No one was injured, but the blast was strong enough to knock down baskets attached to a wall inside the house.

The Boston Globe reported that "the explosion was followed by an anonymous threatening telephone call." Susan's mother, Harriet, reported, "A man said that if we didn't leave town, they would kill us." (This was the second bomb detonated outside the Shapiro's home that week.)

Neither Susan nor her parents have any intention of leaving town.

3

The student editor vs. *the principal*
who tried to shut down the school paper.

A high school principal in New York City had been taken to court by the editor of the student paper. It was the third time in five years that the principal had been forced to defend himself before a federal judge on the charge of illegally censoring the high school newspaper. He had lost on both occasions, and on this morning he had lost again.

Furious, the principal walked toward the elevators. He saw coming toward him—they had left the court by another door—the student and his attorney from the New York Civil Liberties Union. The principal's face reddened and got redder still as his adversaries came nearer. The principal's face got so red that he began to look like Rumpelstiltskin. Pointing a shaking finger at the young attorney, he roared, "You, sir, are inciting this student! You are inciting him to—to exercise his rights!"

The rights of students to a free press are based on a 1969 Supreme Court decision concerning three junior high school students in Des Moines: thirteen-year-old Mary Beth Tinker; her fifteen-year-old brother, John; and a friend of theirs, sixteen-year-old Christopher Eckhardt. They had come to their schools wearing black armbands in protest against the Vietnam War. Ordered to remove the armbands by the principals of the various schools they attended, the three youngsters refused, and were suspended.

The Supreme Court of the United States ruled that the black armbands were a form of speech—symbolic speech. Although no words were used, the armbands symbolized mourning. In this case, mourning for the dead on both sides of what the students felt to be an unjust war. And students, said the Supreme Court, are entitled to express themselves in symbolic or written or verbal speech in school because "It can hardly be argued that either students or teachers shed their constitutional rights to freedom of speech or expression at the schoolhouse gate."

The High Court also said that school authorities could not suppress student expression simply because it might cause trouble. "Any word spoken, in class, in the lunchroom or on the campus, that deviates from the views of another person," said the Court, "may start an argument or cause a disturbance. But our Constitution says we must take this risk . . . and our history says that it is this sort of hazardous freedom—this kind of openness—that is the basis of our national strength and of the independence and vigor of Americans who grow up and live in this . . . often disputatious society."

Ever since that decision, all court rulings affirming the free-press rights of public school students have used *Tinker* as their foundation.

Many students, however, do not know about the *Tinker* decision and about their right to print anything they like, except material that invades the rights of others or by legal definition is obscene or that injures somebody's reputation by libeling him or her. Students also cannot print, according to *Tinker*, articles or editorials or cartoons that may immediately create substantial disorder in the school. It would take some very inflammatory words to do that, and indeed, instances of such explosive material are extremely rare.

With those exceptions, therefore, the student press is quite free, far more than in most countries. But since a lot of students are ignorant of their rights, a good many school officials ignore *Tinker* and censor anything *they* don't like, especially anything that might be controversial. There are other principals, however, who respect the rights of their students.

But when a school is headed by a censor, it takes considerable courage for student journalists to insist on their First Amendment rights. Since 1969 and the *Tinker* decision, there have been a substantial number of student journalists who are real heroes in this regard. One of them is Chuck Reineke.

In 1979, when he was fifteen, Chuck Reineke became a reporter for the *Arrowhead*, the official newspaper at McEachern High School in Cobb County, Georgia. A serious journalist, Reineke went after stories he figured his fellow students had a right to know about. One story pointed out that the principal was violating one of the clauses in the First Amendment about religion by broadcasting daily prayers over the school's public address system. The First Amendment says that an agent of the government (a high school principal, for instance) cannot "establish" or support any religion in a public institution. For instance, a public school cannot, under the Constitution, include organized prayer as part of any school-directed activity.

Reineke's story about the principal's violation of the separation between church and state never appeared in the school paper because a school administrator saw it first.

At the age of sixteen, Chuck Reineke became coeditor of the *Arrowhead*, and his very first issue was confiscated by the principal. (A few copies had been distributed before the principal saw the issue, and he demanded that any student with a copy of those rare *Arrowhead*s turn it over to him. The rest were locked up.)

There were a number of things the principal didn't like in Reineke's first issue as coeditor, particularly a story about a friend of the principal, who had been elected to the board of education. Reineke had found a 1960 ad by the principal's friend in which he had promised "leadership to keep our schools on a segregated basis." Since this part of Georgia was still involved in battles over school integration in 1979, it was responsible journalism for Chuck to print this current school board member's record on segregation.

The principal also objected to an article in the *Arrowhead* attacking Georgia senator Sam Nunn's support of the military draft.

In Chuck Reineke's second issue, he wrote about the principal's confiscation of his first issue. But that article was censored by the faculty adviser.

At last, Chuck Reineke went for help to the American Civil Liberties Union. A young volunteer lawyer for the ACLU, William Hoffman, sent a letter to the school board pointing out that his client's First Amendment rights to freedom of the press were being abused by his principal. Hoffman said that those abuses must stop. The school board ignored his letter, but the principal told Reineke that if he didn't stop causing trouble the *Arrowhead* would be shut down. As a serious journalist, Reineke took the First Amendment seriously, and so he kept on asserting his rights.

The principal shut down the school newspaper.

Reineke went to court. He sued the principal for violating his constitutional rights. On the morning of the hearing before a federal judge in Atlanta, the principal used the school's public address system to beseech the student body to "pray for us as we go to court today."

The judge, G. Ernest Tidwell, started by saying that the school authorities, in order to justify their censorship of the newspaper, had to provide evidence that if the censored articles had been printed they would have disrupted the school. How on earth could that kind of evidence be found?

Well, in an article on Chuck Reineke's case in the March 29, 1980, *Nation*, Michael Simpson, then the director of the Student Press Law Center in Washington—which gives free legal advice to student journalists anywhere in the country—reported that more than one hundred fifty students at the high school signed petitions, conveniently available outside the principal's office, affirming that if those censored articles had been printed the school would have indeed been badly disrupted. Those students wanted to demonstrate their loyalty to the principal, having apparently decided that he was worth more than the First Amendment.

In delivering his opinion, the judge took special note of the *Tinker* decision in 1969 (neither students nor teachers "shed their Constitutional rights to freedom of speech or expression at the schoolhouse gate."). As for the controversy that might have been raised by the articles that were suppressed, the judge quoted from another student free-press court decision: "Speech cannot be stifled by the State merely because it would perhaps draw an adverse reaction from the majority of the people."

As for the statement by more than one hundred fifty students that the school would have exploded if Reineke hadn't been censored, the judge said he didn't believe any such thing. The censored articles, he said, would have just "provoked discussion and comment," and that surely is protected by the First Amendment. They should not have been cut out of the paper, nor should the principal have confiscated an issue of the paper. Furthermore, the principal had acted unlawfully by closing down the paper. School authorities cannot impose censorship, the judge emphasized, by suspending editors, or by withdrawal of financial support, or by shutting a school newspaper down.

In this case, said the judge, not only were the rights of Chuck Reineke and the other workers on the paper violated by the principal, but so were the rights of every student in the school, because they "are being denied the right to . . . receive the information that would have been published in the newspaper."

The court ordered that the paper be immediately restored

to life, and that Chuck Reineke be immediately restored as co–editor in chief of the *Arrowhead*. In addition, the censored articles were to be printed. And the entire issue that had been confiscated by the principal would now be distributed. Finally, there was to be no further censorship of the school paper unless the principal could prove that what he wanted to cut out was, by legal definition, obscene or defamatory, or unless he could show that a certain article would actually cause disruption of the school or serious interference with the rights of students and teachers.

It was a significant victory for Chuck Reineke and for the First Amendment rights of students throughout the country. But the response, among both the majority of adults and students in the Atlanta area, was far from congratulatory. An Atlanta radio station, for example, conducted a poll on the outcome of the case, and its listeners overwhelmingly supported the school principal rather than the courageous student editor.

More sadly, when the confiscated issue of the *Arrowhead* finally appeared five months late, the president of the student body, leading some sixty students, burned a number of copies of the rescued paper in front of the school. The student body president and his followers wanted to demonstrate that they were still loyal to the principal.

As for what Chuck Reineke had learned from his struggle and his ultimate victory, Michael Simpson reported in *The Nation:*

"After he filed suit, many of his classmates reacted with, in his words, 'outright violence.' They called him a 'dirty Commie,' urged him to 'go to Iran,' and telephoned death threats. But [when it was all over, Chuck] was pleased to report that most of the students changed their attitude after reading the released paper. They were surprised that the principal tried to suppress it.

"I really wanted to know," Michael Simpson continued, "how *he* was feeling, whether he carried any bitterness from his on-the-job training with the First Amendment. I asked him whether he was very upset because the student body president torched the *Arrowhead*.

" 'No,' he said simply. 'The purpose of my lawsuit was to win freedom of expression at the McEachern High School, and that freedom includes even the right of students to burn our newspaper if they want to.' "

4

*"Isn't it mature to do the right thing
no matter how hard it may be?"*

Lizette Espana's family comes from El Salvador, and although she was born in San Francisco, Lizette lived amid the death squads and other violence of El Salvador for several years.

At San Jose High School in San Jose, California, she achieved so splendid a record that she was accepted at Yale University and was also to be the valedictorian at her high school graduation exercises in June, 1984.

After the invocation, which spoke of our freedom to express ourselves in America, Lizette Espana delivered only a single line of her speech: "Good afternoon, parents, relatives, friends, teachers and students."

Then, in tears, she announced that school administrators had just removed a page from her six-page script and so she would not go on. After all, the title of her speech was "Images of Orwell." George Orwell was one of this century's most uncompromising opponents of censorship, so how could she possibly "honor" him by reading a speech that had been censored by school authorities?

The full text of her speech was made public, however, after news got around that Lizette had been censored on her graduation day. Her talk was printed by the *San Jose Mercury News*, which also said in an editorial that high school principal

Sam Rodriguez had been "arrogant and foolish" in suppressing a page of Lizette's speech.

If Lizette had given the full text of her speech on graduation day, the students and parents would have heard her say that "the single most frightening event" in George Orwell's *1984* was "the breaking of the human spirit."

The human spirit, she would have gone on, "is being destroyed in El Salvador. . . . When you see friend after friend being murdered, you will listen to and say anything in order to make the pain stop."

Lizette, in her text, went on to credit San Jose High School for her own determination not be broken. The school, she said, made "me into an individual I might not otherwise have become."

But then she felt it necessary to mention some things about the high school that parents might not have known about: an administration that was often too harsh in applying its rules; the presence of incompetent teachers; the departure of good teachers because of tensions in the school caused by the administration.

That was the page that the principal censored.

But Sam Rodriguez bristled at being charged with censorship, a word he says he despises. "I don't think it had anything to do with freedom of speech," the principal told the *San Jose Mercury News*. "There's a fine line between censoring and asking, 'Hey, do you think this is the time or place to say these things?' "

That must be an exceedingly fine line indeed, one that only certain school administrators can see.

In reaction to the printing of Lizette's speech, many people in the area wrote letters to the *Mercury News*. One reader said that Lizette was a quite immature young woman. Lizette leapt right into the debate and said in a letter of her own, "The immature thing for me to have done would have been to buckle under pressure and do what I was told. Isn't it mature to do the right thing no matter how hard it may be?"

But a supporter of principal Sam Rodriguez wrote, "I hope the . . . brains of Yale will wash her down to size with the humility to appreciate the American way of life that she and her own family could not find in her native country."

Around the time the news broke about the censorship of Lizette Espana, a new superintendent of schools, Ramon Cortines, came to town. During a reception for him after his arrival, a number of parents made Cortines aware of what had happened on graduation day to Lizette Espana and George Orwell.

I called the new superintendent and asked him what his own views were.

"Students," said Ramon Cortines, "must grow into adults who contribute to how this society is governed, and there is no other way than free speech for students to learn how to do this.

"From now on," he continued, "if there is nothing libelous or obscene in a student's speech—and there was not in Lizette Espana's talk—it will not be interfered with. I can assure you that the principal and the entire administration staff at San Jose High School, and all the other schools in the district, understand my position."

Meanwhile, a citizen wrote to the _San Jose Mercury News_ in ironic appreciation of principal Sam Rodriguez: "I find myself feeling gratitude to him. Without his censorship, many of us would never have heard of Espana, her ideas, and her ability to express them."

5

*The court orders
remedial classes in the First Amendment
for teachers and administrators.*

In February, 1985, Heidi Webb, a ninth-grader at Montclair High School in San Bernardino County, California, started distributing leaflets between classes. She also did it outside the building before and after school. Her sixth period teacher told her to cease and desist. Heidi Webb asked why. He told her that passing out leaflets was illegal. She asked what law she had broken. He said he'd get back to her.

The student had been handing out literature that surely fits the United States Supreme Court's definition of the "uninhibited, robust" public debate about public issues that is the very core of the First Amendment. Heidi Webb is against abortion, and one of the leaflets she was handing out said: "Killing the innocent is . . . a barbarous approach to problem solving. Its effects on society are no less deadly than its effects on the unborn child."

The next day, the principal confronted Heidi Webb in the school parking lot and ordered her to stop handing out her literature. If she did not stop, she would be expelled for "noncompliance with authority figures."

When her parents called the superintendent of the joint high school district, it was his considered judgment that because of the pamphlets' controversial subject matter, they had no place at school. They should be distributed at a church, on a public sidewalk, or at a teenage discotheque. If Heidi did not obey his orders, the superintendent added, the police would be called.

One day in March during lunch break, while Heidi was giving out pamphlets to students who had asked for them, the vice principal grabbed the rest from her, reprimanded Heidi in front of her schoolmates, and marched her to the principal's office.

That educator, Horace Jackson, suspended Heidi for two days.

On the Parent Notification of Suspension form, the principal explained his action by saying that the young woman had already been warned by him that "the pro-life materials she wanted to distribute were inappropriate, offensive, and inflammatory."

Until that day, Heidi Webb had never been disciplined in any way during her entire school career.

When she returned to school, Heidi Webb kept on distributing the pamphlets because no one, aside from using such adjectives as "inappropriate" and "inflammatory," had told her what law she was breaking. This time she was suspended for four days, and her principal threatened to expel her for the rest of the school year if she persisted in her defiant belief that she, a student, had the First Amendment right to distribute her leaflets.

Heidi Webb's parents contacted the Rutherford Institute, a Christian legal defense group in northern Virginia. One of its attorneys, Larry Crain, filed a lawsuit in the U.S. District Court for the Central District of California. He asked that no further disciplinary measures be taken against Heidi for exercising her First Amendment rights, and that the suspensions be removed from her record.

A lawyer for the school district, Don Haueter, told the *Daily Report* (a San Bernardino County paper) that he thought

Heidi ought to drop the lawsuit. After all, school officials, when they finally asked Haueter for legal advice, had reinstated Heidi Webb. And the principal, Horace Jackson, even wrote her an aplogy for having suspended her. So why continue the lawsuit?

Heidi, however, wanted more than a piece of paper from a repentant principal. "I want to be able to set a precedent," she said. "I don't want them to be able to be sorry and forget about it."

Her lawyer, Larry Crain, agreed. He wanted, and eventually won, an agreement by the school board that what happened to Heidi Webb will not happen again. The First Amendment rights of students to distribute literature will be protected at that school from now on—so long as the time of the distribution doesn't interfere with classroom work, and so long as the material is not legally obscene or defamatory.

Also part of the final settlement of the lawsuit was an agreement by the school district to set up annual workshops on the constitutional free-speech rights of students that will from now on be a regular part of fall orientation sessions at the various schools. Attending those workshops will be principals, administrators, teachers, and students.

This was the first time a court ordered remedial classes in students' constitutional rights for teachers and administrators. The court also awarded Heidi Webb $7,500 in damages for the violation of her First Amendment rights.

II

THE NECESSARY BRAVERY
OF LIBRARIANS

6

*"It would be chilling if a librarian
had to base his or her selection of books
on the basis of what suits everybody."*

Washington County in southwest Virginia is usually a quiet
place, where the big news story of the season is how Abingdon
High School did in the Southwest District football champion-
ship or whether the price for burley tobacco is going up or
down. For most of the people there, religion is a very basic part
of their lives. You can't go far in Washington County without
seeing a church. And politically, most of the people in the
county are firmly conservative.

In 1981, there was a war in Washington County, and before it was over, just about everybody who lived there took
sides in that fierce combat. The war was about what kinds of
books should be in a public library. And the war was also about
what kinds of books should *not* be on the shelves. One preacher
in the county, Tom Williams, wanted to remove from the
Washington County Public Library in Abingdon every book in
it that, according to him, was "filthy" and "pornographic." The
Reverend Williams had a powerful ally, Bobby Sproles, chair-
man of the Washington County Board of Supervisors. That
board had the power to cut the amount of money the library
received each year, and Mr. Sproles felt strongly that if the
library did not get rid of all "questionable" materials, it should
have its funds sharply slashed.

Bobby Sproles and the Reverend Williams also wanted very much to get the library board to fire Kathy Russell, the twenty-three-year-old director of the Washington County Public Library. After all, she was the one who had allowed those "filthy" books into the library. Instead of getting rid of the books, as she had been told to do by the Reverend Williams and Mr. Sproles, this young woman said she did not believe in censorship. She kept reminding her critics that in this country, nobody has a right to police what other people read.

This war of the library was all the more intriguing because it took place in Virginia, the home of James Madison, the principal author of the First Amendment, which guarantees everybody's right to freedom of expression and also, as the Supreme Court has said, the right of everybody to *receive* as well as express ideas. That means our right to receive ideas in books as well as in newspapers and movies and on television.

Virginia was also, of course, the home of Thomas Jefferson, who in 1814, when he heard that a book might be banned because certain authorities objected to its religious views, wrote to a bookseller.

"I am really mortified to be told that, *in the United States of America* . . . [a book] can become the subject of inquiry, and of criminal inquiry too. . . . Are we to have a censor whose imprimatur shall say what books may be sold, and what [books] we may buy? . . . Whose foot is to be the measure to which ours are all to be cut or stretched?"

Here is how the battle of the Washington County Public Library began:

The Reverend Tom Williams walked into the library one day, browsed among the shelves, and made himself a list of books that must be expelled because they were full of "perverted filth." Among them were novels by such widely popular authors as Sidney Sheldon (*Bloodline*), Harold Robbins (*The Lonely Lady*), Philip Roth (*Goodbye, Columbus*), Muriel Davidson

(*The Thursday Woman*), and Jacqueline Susann (*Once Is Not Enough*).

Not only were these and other condemned books to be removed but also, the preacher told Kathy Russell, he wanted the names of every reader who had taken out any of the "pornographic" books on the list. Reverend Williams particularly wanted the names of any young readers who had taken out those books.

Kathy Russell told the preacher that a law of the state of Virginia forbids librarians from telling anybody what books a reader has taken out. And in any case, she continued, even if there had not been such a privacy law on the books, she had always considered such information confidential. Nobody who takes books out of a library should be afraid that somebody might later accuse them of having read "subversive" or "filthy" or "irreligious" books. This is a free nation, Kathy said, and therefore nobody has a right to pry into what other people read.

It was at that point that the Reverend Williams declared war on Kathy Russell. He delivered his denunciations of the librarian and her library in the newspapers, on radio and television stations, in his pulpit, and anywhere else he could get a hearing. And Bobby Sproles also spoke often and harshly about Kathy Russell. What she allowed in the library, Sproles said, "violates the morals of the majority of the people in this country."

As news of the battle spread, reporters from out of state began coming to Washington County. They were told by the natives that Kathy—in her early twenties, slight, soft-voiced, essentially shy—couldn't possibly win this fight. How could she beat both a minister and a powerful county official in so conservative a county? But from the first day of the struggle Kathy Russell was cool, self-assured, and never on the defensive. Wherever her opponents spoke—in the press and on radio and television stations—Kathy immediately asked for and got reply time.

And this is what she said.

In a letter to one local paper, the Bristol *Herald-Courier*, Kathy Russell pointed out that a public library serves *all* the public and therefore, it cannot "enforce the views of any single group in the community as the standard for determining what materials should be made available to everyone in the community."

Furthermore, she kept telling the citizens of Washington County, "It is the responsibility of libraries in the United States to make available materials representing all points of view concerning the questions and issues of our times and reflecting all tastes. . . ."

In answer to the charges that the books on Reverend Williams's list were "pornographic," Kathy Russell said that the only thing those particular books have been found guilty of is having appeared on *The New York Times* list of best sellers. A library cannot exclude books, she said, on the basis that one group of citizens claims that by *their* standards, the books are pornographic.

It is indeed true, Kathy Russell told the *Richmond Times-Dispatch*, that those books on Reverend Williams's list offend some people. And other books in the library offend still other people. But, she emphasized, "It would be chilling if you had to base your selection of books on the basis of what suited *everybody.*"

Think about that. If a decision were made to throw out of the library every book in it that offended *somebody*, what would be left? Maybe some cookbooks, provided they didn't violate some particular religious restrictions on food. And maybe some of Grimms' fairy tales, provided they were not too violent for the taste of some members of the community.

Kathy Russell also underlined, again and again, what freedom to read in this country actually means:

"While anyone is free to reject books for himself, he cannot exercise the right of censorship to restrict the freedom to read of others."

No one, in sum, was forcing Reverend Williams to read any of the books *he* considered so distasteful, but he had no right to prevent other people in the community from reading any books *they* liked, including books that he despised.

A question often asked of Kathy during the war of the library was why taxpayers who objected to the "pornographic" books cited by Reverend Williams should have to see their tax money go to the public library that buys such books.

Kathy's answer was that every one of the so-called pornographic books on the reverend's list was purchased by the library "only after a number of requests for the book were received from regular patrons of the library. They," Kathy emphasized, "pay taxes too." Why should taxpayers be denied the books *they* want to read?

A book that Reverend Williams, in all honesty, considers "filthy" may well be a book that another reader, with different values, considers no more harmful than *Dallas* or *Dynasty* on television.

In any event, during the first weeks of the debate in Washington County, it looked as if Reverend Williams was gathering support. Wrote one retired Baptist minister in a letter to a newspaper, "Stand with me in prayer that this trash will be removed."

A woman whose ancestors have been in southwest Virginia for centuries wrote: "This type of trash [in the library] poisons the minds of our children. No wonder there is so much rape and murder."

But the editor and publisher of the *Washington County News*, Lowry Bowman, also very conscious of the history of Virginia, wrote that the preacher and his politician friend were tarnishing the good name of a place where generations of governors, congressmen, generals, and judges had been born.

"We helped turn the tide of the American Revolution in 1780," Lowry Bowman noted, "and we helped give the world the high ideals of the Bill of Rights"—which begins with the First Amendment.

As the weeks went on, the letters columns in the local dailies and weeklies were bursting with letters about the right-to-read war in Washington County. Gradually, as people had time to think carefully about the issue, a growing proportion of the letters came down in favor of Kathy Russell's insistence that the library was for *everybody.* And accordingly, no one group had the right to take it upon itself to decide what other people should be allowed to read.

Indeed, the letters began to sound like echoes of the debates in eighteenth-century Virginia before the Revolutionary War; debates about independence, including independence of thought.

Said one letter: "This is too much. Way too much. It is time to react to this outrageous impudence and let the self-righteous bigots know that we will not further tolerate having them decide for us what we shall read and what we shall not. . . .

"No one forces these morality experts to go in any bookstore or library and read a single word that offends them. What right have they to assume that because something is offensive to them personally, that material must be proscribed for the rest of us. . . .

"Get off our backs. You read what you want and let me and the others read what we want to."

Agreeing, another letter writer declared, "That's what America is about—freedom. Let's keep it that way."

Still another citizen of Washington County roared, "While I am NOT defending pornography, I AM defending my right to read what I please, and I'll be damned if Mr. Sproles or Mr. Williams is going to tell me that because *they* don't like certain books, others cannot read them."

"If I wanted to submit to Reverend Williams's moral influence," a supporter of Kathy Russell wrote, "I would attend his church. I do not. Yet, he wants to stretch his long arm from the pulpit of that church through the door of the library and yank books from their shelves. This is simply not right."

Newspaper polls were taken to find out who was winning the war. In one of the most conservative districts in Washington County, Kathy was ahead by an eleven to one margin. She did even better in the other districts.

Meanwhile, the Washington County Library Board unanimously backed the librarian, twenty-five hundred citizens signed a petition to keep the library free of censors, and resolutions for support for *everybody's* right to read came from sixteen civic organizations (among them the Kiwanis and Rotary Clubs, Abingdon Jaycees, the Head Start Policy Council, the League of County Voters, and the Washington County Ministerial Association, representing many preachers).

When it was all over, no book had been removed from the library. Nor had the librarian been removed. She later married and left the state, but that was of her own volition, and Kathy left behind for her successor a firm tradition of the library's independence.

Kathy Russell's victory, which was hailed by librarians' associations throughout the country, was the result of her refusal to be intimidated by the would-be censors. She was continually forthright, clear, and especially effective in reminding everyone what it would be like if any one group—whatever its beliefs—were to have the power to decide what books could remain in the library. And what books had to be tossed out.

After Kathy's triumph, I saw her at a meeting of Virginia librarians in Charlottesville. I asked her how rough all of this had been for her.

"It's been difficult at times," she said in the softly falling

rhythms of her native Virginia. "It was hard, you know, during those times when you're by yourself, and you really do
wonder what's going to happen. But I did what I had to do. As
a librarian, I had no choice."

---

7

*"They picked on the wrong person.
I fight back."*

Two years before Kathy Russell conquered the forces of censorship in Washington County, another librarian a long way
from Virginia was fired over the same issue: Does any one seg-
ment of the community have the right to decide which books
are to be denied a place in the local public library?

The place was Davis County, near Salt Lake City in Utah.
It is the most conservative county in the state, and the librarian
in trouble there was Jeanne Layton, director of the Davis
County Libraries in Bountiful, Farmington, and Clearfield. She
had worked for the system for more than twenty years, and had
been director for nine. A conscientious, hard-working professional, Jeanne Layton had lived in the area all her life. She
loved books, the free flow of ideas, and her job.

Jeanne Layton's hard times started in the fall of 1977 when
the parents of a sixteen-year-old boy took a look one night at a
book he had borrowed from the public library. It was a novel,
Americana, by Don DeLillo. As summarized by Lynn Telford
and Louise Kingsbury during an article on Jeanne Layton's
troubles in the October, 1979, *Utah Holiday Magazine*, the novel
"is told in the first person by a 28-year-old television executive.
The narration ruminates on the Vietnam War, corporate power
struggles, the narrator's family relationships, and his sexual ac-

quaintances. Four of the 358 pages describe explicit sexual encounters."

J. Dennis Day, director of the Salt Lake City Libraries and nationally known in library circles for his disdain for would-be censors, described *Americana* as "a well-written book about what is actually happening in our society. . . . Ironically, the author is really a moralist."

The purpose of the book was to show the reader how some of the characters in it had gone wrong—not to hold those characters up as desirable role models.

The parents of the sixteen-year-old boy, however, considered the book to be "filth." People, of course, vary widely in how they react to the same book. As John Harlan, a United States Supreme Court Justice, once said: "One man's vulgarity is another's lyric."

The offended parents took the book to a city councilman in their town, Bountiful City. He too was offended by the book and brought it to the town attorney, who pronounced it obscene and asked the library to remove *Americana* from its shelves.

Instead of banishing the book, Jeanne Layton followed the library's standard procedure. Whenever anyone objected to a book, it was reviewed by a committee of librarians. Jeanne Layton, therefore, appointed a committee, and it found that *Americana* met the criteria of the library's selection policies:

"A book has educational value if it stimulates imagination, develops positive growth, enlarges experience or widens horizons for an individual. . . ."

It is the library's stated policy "to purchase those works of fiction which are well-written and based on authentic human experience."

It is also the library's stated policy not to buy books "which are solely sensational or erotic." The review committee did not judge *Americana* to be that kind of book.

As Jeanne Layton said in a letter to the Bountiful City

Attorney: ". . . the book in total is well-written and presents an honest aspect of modern life, and would positively contribute to an individual's awareness of his/her world."

Americana, Jeanne Layton said, would stay in the library.

There was a certain amount of growling by some of the politicians in the area, but the issue did not become inflamed until nearly a year later, when County Commissioner Morris Swapp became involved. Swapp, a former mayor of Bountiful and a former elementary school principal, was an influential public official who had been appointed to the Davis County Library Board.

Morris Swapp did not believe that the novel *Americana* should be in the public library. Saying that it was "nothing but rot and filth," Swapp demonstrated his contempt for the book by checking it out of one of the branch libraries and stating that he intended never to return it. He did, however, send a check to pay for the book.

That action led to a letter from a frequent library user, Mary C. Corporon, that was published in the Salt Lake City *Deseret News:*

"Mr. Swapp has shown all the people of Utah how to deal with ideas they find offensive. We can all check the books we disagree with out of the library and refuse to return them (paying the appropriate fee for a 'lost book,' of course). Atheists could 'lose' all the books on religion. Republicans could 'lose' all the books espousing Democratic party philosophy. Soon there would be nothing left to offend anyone. . . .

"If *Americana* is really a 'filthy' book, its purveyors should be prosecuted for pornography. And if *Americana* is not pornography, it should be left on the library shelves so that adults may exercise their parental rights to control what their children read without big brother Swapp telling them how to do so."

When the newspapers reported that library board member Morris Swapp had permanently "borrowed" a copy of *Ameri-*

cana, three residents of Utah donated copies of the novel to the Davis County Library, and six more readers offered to give the library copies of *Americana* if they were needed. By that point, there was a long list of library patrons waiting to check out a copy of the book.

Morris Swapp stuck to his guns. And not only was he convinced that *Americana* did not belong in the Davis County Library system, he believed just as firmly that Jeanne Layton didn't belong there either.

This is what happened next, as described by Lynn Telford and Louise Kingsbury in *Utah Holiday Magazine:*

"Once it became clear that Swapp was eager to fire her, she was subjected to what her attorney Albert Colton calls a 'vicious whispering campaign by the opposition.' "

There were rumors that Jeanne Layton is an atheist. She is not; but if she were, is belief in God a requirement for a job as a public librarian? Not under the Constitution of the United States, which forbids any religious test for public employment and also prohibits religious discrimination in private employment.

There was also gossip that Jeanne Layton is a lesbian. She calls that rumor "ludicrous." (And civil libertarians in the state pointed out that in any case, firing someone solely because she is a lesbian is clearly and unfairly discriminatory.)

These and other whispers may have gained some currency because Jeanne Layton lives alone in the conservative town of Kaysville, where she has lived all her life, and because for some twenty years she has not been an active member of the Mormon Church, into which she was born.

All these rumors were started only after Jeanne Layton defended a novel that others in the county wanted to remove from the library.

Her defense, like Kathy Russell's in Virginia, was that as a librarian she had had no choice in acting as she did. Jeanne told Telford and Kingsbury in *Utah Holiday Magazine,* "The library has an obligation to give exposure. Only through exposure can a child grow into a discriminating, selective adult." As for herself, she noted that she is "dedicated to preserving freedom of thought." Jeanne Layton characterizes herself as "a person who stands up for what I believe. I am definitely not a 'yes' person."

Because Morris Swapp had made *Americana* a public issue again, Jeanne Layton appointed a second review committee to read it. That committee also recommended that the novel stay in the library.

In time, two supporters of Swapp replaced members of the library board whose terms had expired, and Swapp had a majority. He asked for Jeanne Layton's resignation. He said *Americana* was not the issue, and presented other accusations instead. But Jeanne Layton had a convincing answer to each of Swapp's new charges, and it seemed to a number of observers that her failure to throw *Americana* out of the library was indeed the real reason she was finally fired in mid-September.

Jeanne Layton fought to get her job back. "They picked on the wrong person," she said. "I fight back." And she added, "I see myself in a position of holding the library together. With me removed, I feel the library has become vulnerable. The new librarian could be so *controlled* that direction to the library staff could be, well . . . manipulated. Frankly, that concerns me." (Emphasis added.)

In a furious editorial, "Davis County Disgrace," the Salt Lake City *Tribune* said, "It isn't necessarily confined to Communist despotism, fascist autocracy, or a banana republic dictatorship. Arbitrary government action can occur under the open canopy of constitutional democracy. That was amply demonstrated in Davis County.

"Making good its intentions to find a scapegoat for a controversy created by Davis County Commissioner Morris F. Swapp, a county library board majority fired County Librarian Jeanne Layton. . . . It was a spectacle difficult to match during the days of Imperial Rome or modern day Tehran. . . .

"Commissioner Swapp contended it all conformed to the doctrine of the 'majority rules.' Not mentioned were the principles of justice, fair play, and protection for individual rights. . . . Personal politics may have triumphed in Davis County. But the good name of constitutional government has been soiled in the process."

The first thing Jeanne Layton did to get her job back was to file an appeal with the Davis County Merit Council, a civil service review panel. She claimed that she had been wrongfully dismissed. She had not been fired because she had been a poor librarian, Jeanne Layton said. She had been fired because she had resisted the censorship of books in her library. But by resisting, Jeanne Layton maintained, she had been faithful to the highest tradition of her profession.

Jeanne Layton was far from alone in her struggle to win back what should never have been taken from her. Librarians from the state of Utah and from the rest of the country rallied around her. In 1979, for the first time in its history, the Utah Library Association censured a library board—that of Davis County, for violating Jeanne Layton's intellectual freedom. And the Freedom to Read Foundation of the American Library Association helped pay Jeanne Layton's legal fees.

Meanwhile, Jeanne Layton went into Federal Court and sued the three-member majority of the library board that fired her. She charged them with not only abusing her own constitutional rights but also the right of Davis County citizens to read controversial literature, protected by the First Amendment.

On the other hand, one group in the state of Utah, Citizens for True Freedom, was delighted that Jeanne Layton had been fired. Citizens for True Freedom was devoted to improving the morality of bookstores and libraries throughout the state, and that meant removing "immoral" books and other materials.

When Layton was fired, Joy Beech, director of Citizens for True Freedom, predicted that from now on, "there will be quite a few books removed from the library. Now that people know they have a conservative board, more people will present books to the board."

Citizens for True Freedom was about to be terribly disappointed. On January 14, 1980, Jeanne Layton won her job back, including all the salary she had lost. The Davis County Merit Council ruled unanimously that she had been fired without cause.

But the fight wasn't over yet. Morris Swapp and the rest of the majority of the library board ordered the county attorney to appeal the decision.

By that point, Jeanne Layton's legal bills were more than $33,000. In announcing a campaign among librarians around the country to help her raise that money, J. Dennis Day, president of the Utah Library Association, said:

"Jeanne has laid her job and her resources on the line. *She is fighting a battle for all of us.* What are *you* going to do?"

The money came in from librarians in Utah and other states. Meanwhile, the appeal of her opponents on the Davis County Library Board to get her fired again was denied by a superior court in the state of Utah.

In December, 1982, Jeanne Layton won her final victory. In an out-of-court settlement of her federal case against the library board for violating her constitutional rights, the determined librarian was awarded $50,000 in legal fees, which had continued to mount.

A couple of years after her victory, I saw Jeanne Layton at a meeting of the American Library Association's Freedom to Read Foundation in Los Angeles. Sitting at the back of the room, she was introduced to great applause, and smiling, Jeanne said nothing. She didn't have to say anything. Her successful resistance to the censors in Davis County had said it all. And because of that resistance, she has more authority as director of the libraries of Davis County than she ever had before. Part of the agreement settling her lawsuit is that she will never again be dismissed arbitrarily. The library board will have to show legitimate cause for the firing—a cause that can stand up in court.

What happened to Jeanne Layton's chief opponent, the fierce Morris Swapp? Well, after Layton regained her job, Swapp was badly defeated for the Republican renomination to the county commission (a position that had enabled him to sit on the library board). His defeat was partly due to what he tried to do to Jeanne Layton. But it was also caused, Davis County residents say, by his otherwise having offended a lot of people by his arbitrary ways. Most of the people in the county are conservative, but they set great store by whether a public official treats everyone alike.

Swapp finally got a post on a commission charged with abating the nuisance of mosquitoes. In a way, he may be more comfortable in that job, because at one meeting concerning the purchase of library books he attended while on the library board, Swapp said he couldn't even pronounce the titles, so "we have no business putting them in the library if we can't pronounce them. Nobody would want them."

The titles to which he was referring were those of some of the basic, standard works of Eastern religions.

For a long time in this Davis County war, it had seemed as though Morris Swapp would prevail. Jeanne Layton and the First Amendment won, however, because, like Kathy Russell in Washington County, Virginia, she and her supporters fought back hard, with clarity, and with particular attention to letting the newspapers and the radio and television stations know exactly what the issues were. They didn't let Morris Swapp and his allies take the play away from them at any point.

Getting to the citizens of Davis County and the rest of the state was vital because Jeanne Layton had to win more than the legal battle. She and her supporters had to convince as many people as they could of the dangers to *their* First Amendment right to read, if librarians could be fired for refusing to be censors. If she had failed to do that, even if she'd won a court victory, there wouldn't have been enough public support for the principles of her fight, and another Morris Swapp could go after other books later.

Particularly effective in making the issues clear to the people of Davis County and the state of Utah were television programs that enabled viewers to actually see and hear both Morris Swapp and his allies, and the supporters of Jeanne Layton.

On *Crossfire*, a program on KTVX, Salt Lake City, for example, a woman from Czechoslovakia in the studio audience spoke about how the Communist authorities in that country often forbade the reading of books. Having lived in a country in which this took place, she urged Americans to realize what censorship could do to this country.

Another woman in the audience said forcefully that she was a regular user of the Davis County Public Library and that she certainly did have a right to choose what books she wanted to read, "and nobody is going to take that right away from me!"

III

THE DAY
THE POLICE DOGS
SEARCHED EVERY KID
IN SCHOOL

8

*"Being a teenage schoolgirl is neither
a crime nor a cause for suspicion."*

About thirty thousand people live in Highland, in the north-
west corner of Indiana. In addition to several elementary
schools, Highland has a junior and a senior high school. The
latter two school buildings are next to each other, and the 2,780
students of both schools share common facilities.

In 1979, one of the junior high school students was thirteen-year-old Diane Doe. (That is not her real last name but as
you are about to see, her classmates and her neighbors did
know her real last name during Diane's long court battle for
her right to privacy, even in school.)

On March 23, 1979, Diane went to school as usual. Her
first class started at 8:20 A.M., and on every day until this one, it
had ended at 9:15. This morning, however, the class did not
end until 11:45.

Around 9:15, the teacher told Diane and the twenty-seven
other students that the class was going to be held over because
the school had a "surprise" for the students.

A few minutes later, there came to the door of the classroom a German shepherd dog, a dog handler, two policemen in
uniform, and an assistant principal of the junior high school.
They were one of six teams that were conducting raids on all
the classrooms in the junior and senior high schools that
morning.

For the next two hours, Diane Doe and her classmates, like the students in all the other rooms in both schools, were ordered to sit motionless in their seats. Their hands had to be on their desks for the whole time, and the contents of their desks had to be outside, in plain view. All purses had to be on the floor between the students' feet. No one was allowed to go to the bathroom without an escort.

This was indeed quite a surprise for the students. The reason for the raid, according to Superintendent of Schools Omer Renfrow, was "to see if there were any drugs present" in the schools of Highland. During the preceding six months, there had been twenty-one instances of students found in possession of alcohol, drugs, or drug paraphernalia. (About 0.75 percent of the campus population had been involved.)

Some school officials had also received anonymous letters and phone calls, student tips, and information from teachers about alleged drug abuse in the schools. To relieve the concerns of some parents and to deter any future drug abuse in the classrooms of Highland, the superintendent worked out the idea for the raids with police officials and with a professional trainer of police dogs. Each student was to be closely examined by a police dog, and if the dog showed particular interest in him or her, the dog handler would consider this an "alert" that marijuana or some other unlawful substance had been found on the student.

Any student given this special attention by a police dog would be questioned by the authorities. Boys would have to empy their pockets and girls their purses. Moreover, if the dog handler gave the order, kids whom the dogs had sniffed with particular enthusiasm would have to take off their clothing and submit to body searches in the nude.

While the dog detectives prowled the aisles of the Highland classrooms, all the doors of the school buildings were either locked or carefully guarded by police and school officials. Any students who were late for the first class of the day—along

with any visitors to the school during the hours of the raid—
were to be confined in a special room set aside for that purpose.

It should be noted that in making their elaborate plans for
the raid, neither school nor police officials had any specific information that any specific student might be involved in any
unlawful activity concerning drugs or alcohol. No one conducting the raid had been given the names of any particular
students to be particularly questioned or searched. *Every one of
the 2,780 students was regarded as a suspect, even though there wasn't
any specific evidence or reasonable suspicion connecting any one of them
to drug use.*

Yet according to the American system of justice, as we all
learn in school—or are supposed to learn in school—everyone
is presumed innocent until proved guilty.

Uniformed police officers were stationed in the halls of
both schools that morning to make sure no one interfered with
the special education that was going on in the classrooms. In-
vited to watch and report on the raid were journalists from
newspapers and television; those conducting the raid were
proud of their accomplishment, and wanted the public to know
about it too.

"The dogs"—as Supreme Court Justice William Brennan
was later to describe the events of that morning—"were led up
and down each side of the classroom from desk to desk, and
from student to student. Each student was probed, sniffed, and
inspected by at least one of the 14 German shepherds detailed
to the school."

When the German shepherd who took charge of Diane's
classroom reached her, the police dog pressed forward, sniffed
her body, ran its cold nose up her bare leg, under her skirt, and
between her legs. The dog did this repeatedly. The dog had
sounded an "alert" on Diane.

A cop ordered the thirteen-year-old to stand and empty
her purse. No drugs were found. The dog sniffed Diane's body
again, and once more "alerted." At that point a cop ordered

Diane to the nurse's office, to which she was escorted by a male teacher. There she was to get a more thorough physical examination—much more thorough. As she left, some of her classmates giggled and snickered, imagining what was in store for her.

At the nurse's office, Diane was turned over to a female uniformed police officer and to another woman, who was an acquaintance of her mother. Diane denied that she had ever used marijuana or any other drug in her whole life. The women commanded the girl to take off all her clothing, and Diane did. The woman examined her whole body, touched and examined her hair, and inspected her clothing while Diane stood there, nude, shocked, and embarrassed.

No drugs were found on Diane. She returned to her classroom to be greeted by more winks and snickers from some of the other students. In the days after, Diane was aware that not only her classmates but other members of the Highland community were whispering about her and speculating that since she had been subjected to a nude search, the cops must have had something on her.

Diane became angrier and angrier at what had happened to her. So did her parents. She comes from a very traditional Mexican-American family that is strongly conservative in its religious, political, and social beliefs. There had been no history of drug usage in the entire family, very much including Diane. Indeed, throughout her entire school career, Diane had never been suspected by anyone of being involved with drugs. Yet she had now been searched by a police dog and then in the nude by a police officer. And nothing had been found.

(Why had the police dog "alerted" when it searched Diane? She had a dog of her own and that morning, before going to school, Diane had been playing with her pet. Her dog was in heat, and it was *that* smell, which lingered on Diane when she went to school, that caused the police dog to make a false alert.)

A number of the other students and their parents were

outraged at the raid, but eventually only Diane went to court to sue various Highland school officials, the police chief, and the trainer of the German shepherds used during the search. Diane's right to privacy had been abused, she had been humiliated, and she wanted to prevent this ever happening again to kids in her school and other schools. It was just plain un-American for everyone in a school to be held as a suspect, with no one being told of his or her constitutional rights.

Not a single Highland student had been advised of his or her rights to privacy under the Fourth Amendment before, during, or after the raid. Nor did the police go to a judge for search warrants before entering the classrooms with the dogs.

Clearly, there were many important issues in this case, for students throughout the country. And Diane, very much aware that going to court would make her the object of further public attention and embarrassment in Highland, nonetheless decided to go through with it. As one of her lawyers, Joseph A. Morris, told me, "She is a very brave girl."

Before going with Diane on her journey through the law courts, how successful—whether or not it violated the students' Constitutional rights—was the raid?

In the junior high school, the police dogs "alerted" to twenty students. Four, all of them female, were removed from their classes, stripped nude, and interrogated. Nothing illegal was found on any of them. Nor was anything illegal discovered on the sixteen other junior high school students whom the dogs had found to be suspicious.

In the high school, five students—three of them female and two male—were taken out of their classrooms and subjected to extensive, although non-nude, body searches. None of the five was in possession of any unlawful material.

When it was all over, out of 2,780 Highland students who were detained in their classrooms and sniffed by dogs, only seventeen were found to have broken the law. They were high school seniors, and among them were found marijuana, drug "paraphernalia," and three cans of beer.

As Diane Doe's lawyers were to ask during her long battle, which went all the way to the Supreme Court: was this mass search by the police and by the Highland school authorities justified under the Constitution of the United States? And furthermore, were the nude searches—the strip searches, as they're called—of the four junior high school students, including Diane, lawful? Or did the police and school authorities themselves break the law in authorizing and conducting those nude searches?

Consider what happened that day, as described by Diane's attorneys: ". . . disruption of schooling; the terror of arrest and detention; the intrusion of probing dogs; the spectacle of school children being treated as if they were inmates of a prison; the humiliation of being singled out as a suspected criminal; and the indignity of submission to strip searches and other intrusions."

But don't police and school officials have the right—indeed, the responsibility—to do everything they can to stop the use of drugs and alcohol in school? Of course they do—provided their methods do not violate the Constitution of the United States. The essence of Diane's case was that the raid had flagrantly violated her own Fourth Amendment rights and those of every other student in the junior high and high schools.

What does the Fourth Amendment actually say? How did we come to have a Fourth Amendment in this country? And why was it so important to the citizens of the new nation?

A brutal element of British rule that made the colonists especially furious was the "writs of assistance"—general search warrants—which allowed officers of the king to invade any home in search of goods on which the heavy British taxes had not been paid. And sometimes the British agents would burst through the door in search of pamphlets and other literature critical of the king and members of his government. Armed with one of those general search warrants, the British troops could shatter any colonist's privacy at will.

A particularly fiery and effective opponent of these humiliating searches by British agents was James Otis, a Massachusetts lawyer. Indeed, Otis so stirred up the colonists about the British contempt for the privacy of their homes that later John Adams, our second President, said that the "Child Independence, was born" when Otis began to lead the fight against the general search warrants. "Otis," Adams recalled, "was a flame of fire!"

Listen, for instance, to this letter to the colonists in 1772 from a committee that included Otis and Samuel Adams: "Thus our houses and even our bed chambers are exposed to be ransacked. Our boxes, chests, and trunks broke open, ravaged and plundered by wretches, whom no prudent man would venture to employ as menial servants. . . . By this we are cut off from that domestic security which renders the lives of the most unhappy in some measure agreeable. . . ."

So the Fourth Amendment was a direct result of the colonists' fierce anger at being unable to protect themselves and their property from brutal, arbitrary searches by agents of the crown. With that anger still very much alive, the newly independent Americans insisted that this Amendment, the Fourth, be added to the Constitution:

> The right of the people to be secure in their persons, houses, papers and effects, against unreasonable searches and seizures, shall not be violated, and no warrants shall issue, but upon probable cause, supported by oath or affirmation, and particularly describing the place to be searched, and the persons to be searched.

That means, first of all, that neither we nor our houses can be searched, or our wallets or purses gone through, by the police, unless a law-enforcement officer has first gone to a judge and convinced the judge that there is probable cause to believe that a search of this particular person and this particular place will disclose certain particular evidence that a crime has been committed.

As for what happened to Diane Doe and the other students in the Highland schools the day of the raid, did a judge issue a warrant for the search? No judge did.

Did the authorities have a list of particular students and particular places to be searched, or was this the kind of *general* search that had so enraged the American colonists? Obviously, it was a general search.

As Diane's lawyers said:

"The Highland authorities knew nothing in particular about any student, except that he (or she) was present, together with his (or her) thousands of fellows, in a school in which the authorities vaguely suspected that a few students might occasionally possess illicit drugs." Therefore, Diane went to court to directly challenge "a conspiracy of law enforcement and school officials who, however well-intentioned they may be, have converted public school houses into police checkpoints."

Sounding like a modern-day James Otis, Diane's attorneys charged that the police and school authorities "have subjected thousands of students to indiscriminate mass detention, and have searched students without probable cause. Probable cause requires the presence of particularized facts which justify the search of a specific individual in a specific place at a specific time. . . . Diane Doe and her fellow students committed no crimes and no overt acts which could possibly give rise to probable cause for an arrest and search.

". . . The school and police authorities admit that both in the days prior to the dog search, and at the commencement of the raid itself, they possessed absolutely no specific information, derived from any sources whatsoever, concerning any particular drugs or contraband [illegal material], any particular transactions or events, or any particular drug suppliers or abusers. When the drug raid was executed, the participating school and police authorities and their helpers were given the names of no particular students to be watched, searched, or interrogated. *All 2,780 students were treated as equally suspect.*" (Emphasis added.)

What the police and the officials had lost sight of was that *"being a teenaged schoolgirl is neither a crime nor a cause for suspicion."* (Emphasis added.)

Diane's lawyers also reminded the court of what Supreme Court Justice Robert Jackson said in 1949 about our Fourth Amendment rights as Americans. (The date is significant because Justice Jackson had recently returned to the Supreme Court after serving as a prosecutor of Nazi war criminals at the Nuremberg Trials.) Wrote Jackson:

"These [Fourth Amendment rights], I protest, are not mere second-class rights but belong in the catalogue of indispensable freedoms. Among deprivations of rights, none is so effective in cowing a population, crushing the spirit of the individual and putting terror in every heart. Uncontrolled search and seizure is one of the first and most effective weapons in the arsenal of every arbitrary government."

In justification of what they had done, however, the school authorities argued that if the principal had walked into any part of the school and had smelled something with an odor like that of marijuana, surely he would have been justified in searching the person from which that odor was coming.

In answer, Diane Doe's attorney said:

"If we are to understand the dogs' muzzles as mere extensions of the nostrils of the principal, then Highland's school administrators have been sticking their noses into some singular places. The dogs ran their noses along pupils' legs, between their shoes, and even into their crotches and buttocks, actually touching the bodies of the students. Surely it can be vouchsafed that no respectable school administrator would do the same."

9

*"Schools cannot expect their students
to learn the lessons of good citizenship
when the school authorities themselves
disregard the fundamental principles
underpinning our constitutional
freedoms."*

At first, Diane Doe was not alone in her court battle to teach school and police authorities that American students should not be treated as if they have no Fourth Amendment rights. She had initially been joined by nine other students and their parents; but by the time of the trial in federal district court in Hammond, Indiana, only Diane was left. The other families had abandoned the case for various reasons, including the fear that people in the community who wanted tough measures against drugs in schools would retaliate against them if they tried to punish the police and school officials for the drug raid.

And indeed, there was negative reaction in the community to Diane and her parents for having the effrontery to make a court case out of a conscientious attempt to catch students who were drug users. Worse yet, some people claimed, Diane was giving the school and the town a bad name by charging that its officials had trampled the students' constitutional rights.

Diane and her parents, however, were determined to go all the way to the Supreme Court of the United States, if necessary. And they wanted money damages to pay for the hurt and humiliation Diane had suffered.

After the trial in 1979, federal district judge Allen Sharp ruled against Diane on all but one part of her complaint. It was okay to have held the students in custody in their classrooms well past the end of the first period, said the judge. And there was nothing wrong with the presence of uniformed police in the school as part of the school-wide search. Both strategies, the judge declared, were legitimate exercises by school officials of their responsibility to keep the school safe and to make sure that no illegal activities were taking place in the school.

The judge also saw nothing wrong in having the dog handlers and the dogs come into the classrooms. The dogs, he said, were only providing help to the inferior human senses of the school officials through their superior ability to detect the smell of marijuana. And anyway, having a dog sniff at you is by itself not a search as defined by the Fourth Amendment, the judge went on.

Furthermore, Judge Sharp said, kids in school don't have full Fourth Amendment rights.

He then dealt with the charge by Diane's lawyers that because school officials had no specific drug-related information about specific students, there was no "probable cause" for *any* Highland student to have been searched during the raid.

Judge Sharp disagreed. When you're talking about a school and the duty of the people in charge to keep it safe and orderly, he said, you can't impose the high standard of "probable cause" —the need to have particular information about particular people—before a search can be conducted. School officials have to be allowed a lower standard by which they can search. If they have "reasonable cause to believe" that something funny is going on, even if they don't know who may be involved, that's all school officials need before moving in on the kids. Under that lower standard, a warrant from a judge is not necessary for the search to go on.

In only one respect did Judge Sharp believe that Diane's constitutional rights had been violated. She should not have been subjected to a nude search. That kind of search, which is so fundamental an intrusion into an individual's privacy, cannot be based simply on a dog's "alert." Why? Because the dog is not reacting to the drug itself but only to its smell; and a student's clothing might have been exposed to that odor without the student being either a user or seller of marijuana. (Or, as in the case of Diane, the police dog could be reacting to the smell on the student's clothing of another dog in heat, and not to marijuana at all.)

The judge admitted that the school authorities had had no reason whatever to believe that Diane was involved with drugs, so the basically intrusive nude search did indeed "violate her Fourth Amendment right against an unreasonable search and seizure." He had no objections to the police dog sniffing her and going up her leg while she was seated at her desk, but the subsequent strip search was too intrusive. It went too far.

Even so, said the judge, Diane was not entitled to any money damages for the humiliation and other emotional distress she experienced as a result of the nude search. The school authorities had said they had been acting in good faith, trying to keep the school safe, and so they were immune from being punished. The judge agreed with the school authorities that they had not intended to do wrong.

At the very end of his decision, Judge Sharp made note that Diane, by coming forward to press her constitutional rights, was not engaging in an entirely popular action in her hometown. "It is also very clear from the record," the judge wrote, "that some students in the high school are not in sympathy with the claims and contentions of this plaintiff." Indeed, two Highland students testified during the trial that they supported the dog raid. And many other students agreed with them, not with Diane.

Nonetheless, Diane, although she had lost in this court,

kept on, moving now to the Court of Appeals for the Seventh Circuit of the United States. (If she lost there, her last resort would be the United States Supreme Court.)

At the court of appeals, Diane failed to persuade the majority of the judges that her cause was just, except with regard to the nude search.

The majority agreed with the federal district court that there had been nothing wrong with the classroom detention of every student; that the sniffing of the trained police dogs was not a search as the Fourth Amendment defines searches; and that the school district, using the lower standard of "reasonable cause to believe" there was drug activity at Highland, had engaged in a lawful mass search.

However, the judges disagreed with the district judge, Allen Sharp, that school officials could not be sued for damages because of the nude search of Diane. The school authorities may have acted in good faith, said the court of appeals, but they acted in such ignorance of the Fourth Amendment in authorizing the nude search that they could not be immune from an action for damages. As school officials, they are expected to know better. Thinking about that nude search, the Court of Appeals became quite angry:

> It does not require a constitutional scholar to conclude that a nude search of a thirteen-year-old child is an invasion of constitutional rights of some magnitude.
>
> More than that: it is a violation of any known principle of human decency. Apart from any constitutional readings and rulings, simple common sense would indicate that the conduct of the school officials in permitting such a nude search was not only unlawful but outrageous under "settled indisputable principles of law." . . .
>
> *We suggest as strongly as possible that the conduct herein described exceeded the "bounds of reason" by two and a half country miles.* (Emphasis added.)

The question of how much Diane would get in damages was sent back to the first court, the federal district court in Indiana. But Diane still wouldn't give up on the rest of her case. Accordingly, she appealed to the United States Supreme Court. For the nation's highest court to listen to an appeal, four of the nine justices have to say they want to hear the case.

Diane could not persuade four Justices to listen to her arguments. But one of them, Justice William Brennan, was so enraged at what had happened to her that he did a rather rare thing. Usually, when the Supreme Court declines to hear an appeal we never know how many, if any, justices did want to give that particular case a last chance. All we know is that fewer than four wanted to hear it. But once in a while, a member of the Court is so incensed at his colleagues' refusal to review a case that he or she writes a public dissent to bring attention to the issue.

Justice Brennan began his public dissent by saying that Diane was right—all the way:

> I cannnot agree that the Fourth Amendment authorizes local school and police officials to detain every junior and senior high school student present in a town's public schools and then, using drug-detecting, police-trained German shepherds, to conduct a warrantless, student-by-student dragnet inspection "to see if there were any drugs present."
>
> While school officials acting in loco parentis [in place of the parent] may take reasonable steps to maintain a safe and healthful educational environment, *their actions must nonetheless be consistent with the Fourth Amendment. The problem of drug abuse in the schools is not to be solved by conducting schoolhouse raids on suspect students [without] particularized information regarding drug users or suppliers.* (Emphasis added.)

Or, as Diane's lawyers had said of the school officials, "The worthiness of their goals and the drama of the plan so consumed them that, in the secret urgency of it all, they discarded any respect for constitutional restraint."

But what about the dogs? Both lower courts had ruled that what the police dogs did to Diane and the other students was not a search as the Fourth Amendment defines a search.

Of course the dogs were searching the students, said Justice Brennan:

"The dogs were led from student to student for the express purpose of sniffing their clothing and their bodies to obtain information that the school authorities and police officers, with their less developed sense of smell, were incapable of obtaining." And as for Diane, "the dog repeatedly jabbed its nose into her legs. [She] testified that the experience of being sniffed and prodded by trained police dogs in the presence of the police and representatives of the press was degrading and embarrassing.

"I am astonished that the court did not find that the school's use of the dogs constituted an invasion of [her] reasonable expectation of privacy."

Furthermore, said Justice Brennan, not only school officials conducted the search; police were along too. And any time a police officer makes a search, outside a school or inside it, he must be held to the highest constitutional standard there is—probable cause. He must have advance knowledge of particular people and places to be searched. When they went on the raid, the cops had no such particularized information: "The authorities had no more than a generalized hope that their sweeping investigative techniques would lead to the discovery of contraband."

Finally, Justice Brennan thundered:

"We do not know what class [Diane Doe] was attending when the police and dogs burst in, but the lesson the school authorities taught her that day will undoubtedly make a greater impression than her teacher had hoped to convey. . . .

"Schools cannot expect their students to learn the lessons

of good citizenship when the school authorities themselves disregard the fundamental principles underpinning our constitutional freedoms."

Although the Supreme Court would not hear her appeal, Diane's fight was not over. The Court of Appeals had agreed that she was entitled to damages for her nude search, and back in Indiana, the school and police authorities finally made a settlement with Diane's lawyers. One of the terms of the settlement was an agreement that the amount of the money Diane won was not to be publicly disclosed. Yet a person close to the case has told me that "the money is enough to take care of her undergraduate and graduate tuition, including living expenses, at a very good university."

From the beginning of the lawsuit, Diane's parents had insisted Diane's real last name not be used on the court papers because they feared she'd be exposed to ridicule or even to demonstrations by people who had been in favor of the massive drug raid with the dogs. But the students in her school knew who she was, as did the people in her neighborhood. Diane, however, never retreated, testifying and being cross-examined in open court.

Diane didn't win everything she'd wanted, but she did win damages for the unconstitutional nude search she had undergone, and she regained her self-respect by fighting all the way to protest what had been done to her.

A while ago, Supreme Court Justice William Brennan said he was greatly troubled "that so many Americans fail to understand the deeper meaning of the Bill of Rights. I do not suggest," Brennan added, "that students cannot recite the text of the first ten amendments. On the whole that seems to be done quite smoothly. What does concern me deeply is that the impact of the words of the Bill of Rights very often fails to get off the printed page and into real life."

For Diane Doe, the printed page—particularly the Fourth Amendment—has indeed become an important part of her real life.

IV

THE NONVIOLENT
REVOLUTIONARY

10

*"I'll tell you who's impractical and escapist—
anybody who thinks we're going to survive
this century if we continue as we are."*

During the worst of times for Susan Shapiro—daily threats of getting beaten up at school; most of the students not speaking to her; and anti-Semitic threats at home, in the mail and on the phone—she was visited by an internationally famous singer.

Joan Baez was in the Boston area at the time, read about the attacks on Susan, called her up, and went to see the seventeen-year-old at her home in Randolph. Joan admires people who stick by their principles. She herself had stopped saluting the flag in school when she was sixteen and that same year had refused to leave school with her classmates during an air-raid drill because of her total opposition to war and preparations for war. Joan went on to become not only a compelling performer but also a world-renowned nonviolent revolutionary working for an end to all wars, as well as an end to the torture and imprisonment of people of conscience throughout the globe.

Bob Dylan once wrote that Joan's voice was "like gypsy drums an' Chinese gongs an' cathedral bells an' tones 'f chimes. . . . It just held hymns 'f mystery."

When, at the age of eighteen, she first became a magnetic national figure at the 1959 Newport Folk Festival, a critic spoke of Joan's "achingly pure soprano," and *Time* magazine said,

"Her voice is as clear as air in the autumn . . . vibrant, strong, untrained and thrilling."

She was singing folk songs then, but after a while, as she got to know Bob Dylan, she also included his songs in her concerts. And soon—because he was not yet as well known as she was—Joan included Bob in her appearances in order to widen his audience.

Joan, after Dylan had leapt to his own stardom, could have continued making a lot of money on her own with her luminous sound and her centuries-old ballads of doomed lovers, silver daggers, and runaway passions. But she felt impelled to become a part of her own time, musically and politically. She found it was getting harder to remain silent when she learned of an injustice.

In 1963, for example, Joan first became controversial when she refused to appear on a very popular television music series, ABC-TV's *Hootenanny*. She wouldn't go on because she discovered that ABC had refused to let Pete Seeger, one of the best-known folksingers in the country, appear on the show. The network ruled that Seeger's political associations were too "controversial"—that is, he was considered a left-winger. Joan said that if Seeger was going to be punished for his views in this land of the free, the least she could do by way of protest was to refuse to go on that cowardly program.

The next year, Joan engaged in another kind of protest. Opposed to America's involvement in the war in Vietnam, she started refusing to pay that part of her income taxes which, as she figured it out, would be used for the military machinery of death. The government, of course, kept collecting that money —with interest—from her bank accounts, but Joan wanted to make that kind of public statement against the war.

During the rest of the 1960s, Joan, far more than any other performer, was on the front line of nonviolent action against injustice. She marched and sang for civil rights in the South, sometimes alongside Martin Luther King, and she also

marched and sang in the North. In the West, she helped Cesar
Chavez organize farmworkers who had been cheated and denied decent wages and housing for their families all their lives.

And whatever else she was doing, Joan battled—nonvi-
olently—against war. In October, 1967, she was arrested with
one hundred eighteen others for blocking the Armed Forces
Induction Center in Oakland, California; and after serving a
ten-day sentence at Santa Rita Prison Farm, she was arrested
again in December for sitting in in front of the Oakland induction center. The result was another prison term, this one for
thirty-one days.

Joan also kept on singing, but as she often said, "Music
alone isn't enough for me. If I'm not on the side of life in action
as well as in music, then all those sounds, however beautiful,
are irrelevant to the only real question of this century: How do
we stop men from murdering each other, and what am I doing
with my life to help stop the murdering?"

As long as she can remember—"since I was a little girl"—
Joan Baez has been against violence. Even as a child, "I knew
that I didn't have the right to do injury to anyone."

Also, as a dark-skinned little girl—daughter of a Mexican-
American father, a physicist, and a Scottish-American mother
—Joan was sometimes taunted, and she experienced other
forms of racial prejudice. She didn't know the term "civil
rights" then, but she knew what it felt like to be excluded.

Joan's insistence that nonviolence is the only way any of us
can survive was underlined in what she said during a concert
in Holland in 1977 for the International Fellowship of Recon-
ciliation, a pacifist group:

"I expect to spend the rest of my life defining nonviolence,
which is the opposite of passivity. I would say that I'm a nonviolent soldier—which means that in place of archaic, reaction-
ary, stupid weapons of violence, you have to use your mind,
your heart, your sense of humor, every faculty that's available
to you. And if it's not available to you, you have to find it,

because no one has the right to take the life of another human being."

Later, she added, "No one has the right to do injury to another person or to be an accomplice in the doing of injury. This means you have to recognize that everybody is equal and there's no such thing as an enemy. . . . The term *enemy* just gets in the way of understanding that we are all human beings."

Because she has been utterly consistent in her life as a nonviolent soldier—whether protesting killings by her own nation, by right-wing dictatorships or by Communist countries—I once asked Joan a series of difficult questions about nonviolence. For instance, had she ever been in a situation where she was actually able to stop violence through her own nonviolence?

Her answer, in a *Playboy* interview I did with her:

> One of the times I was in prison, there was a girl who had already done six months, waiting to find out what her sentence would be. She had no money and there was no lawyer working for her. She just sat there waiting to appear in court. And when she finally did get sentenced, the time she'd been waiting wouldn't count; it just wouldn't come off her sentence.

> Periodically, she used to get just furious and pick a fight with somebody. She was a black girl, and one time she picked a fight with a white girl from the kitchen. I knew the white girl was a nonfighter; so I went over to try to talk to the black girl. "Get out of my way!" she said. But I stayed where I was standing, so that she couldn't move unless she kicked me aside. She didn't want to kick me. She had hold of the white girl's hair and was trying to kick her in the stomach, and there I was—in the way.

> Finally, her kicks got milder and then she exploded in tears. And I hugged her. You see, I *did* something. I got in the way. Nonviolently. . . . To be part of this kind of

[nonviolent] fighting, you have to be forceful; you have to be aggressive.

But not so aggressive that you slide over into violence, for "when you do violence to another, you're also doing violence to yourself; you're diminishing your own humanity. That's true even when it's just the rhetoric—the language—of violence you're indulging in."

I asked Joan about the charges by her critics that her non-violent approach is impractical, naive, escapist.

"Is it impractical, naive, or escapist," she answered, "to act against violence when we're on the edge of World War II? I'll tell you who's impractical and escapist—anybody who thinks we're going to survive this century if we continue as we are. *That* person is impractical and naive and foolish."

But what can any *one* person do?

"A very basic and sane beginning is to decide to live in such a way that you're not exploiting or damaging somebody else. We all have in us, on the one hand, stupidity, fear, greed, and a lot of other destructive qualities. But on the other hand, there are elements of decency and kindness and love. The question is, which elements in us are we going to nurture?"

Joan Baez has no fear of speaking her mind, no matter what the situation. She was talking once on a college campus about how to organize for peace when a number of black radicals tried to shout her down.

"Hey, hold it!" she shouted back. "I've just got one thing to say: do you have any interest in hearing what I have to say?"

"NO!" they roared back.

"That's just what I thought," Joan said, and everybody laughed, including a couple of the hecklers.

The humor made the lead shouter feel a little uncomfortable, and so, when Joan started to speak again, he didn't interrupt. As for what happened then, Joan recalls:

"The man who'd been doing the shouting had been talking

insultingly about Irish this and Jewish that and Italian the other thing. What I said was, 'Listen, if you're going to end racism, you're going to have to stop *being* a racist. You're going to have to stop putting people in groups.'

"I mean, how can you be part of real change unless you see, or try to see, each person in terms of who he is? When I say you can't end racism if you're a racist yourself, I'm also trying to show that you can't make a new kind of society by forgetting that every one of us is valuable and unique, that the most important thing—before all others—is the sanctity of each human life."

I asked Joan if she ever gets discouraged.

"Sometimes. Like when a woman said to me, 'You're all by yourself. How do you go on thinking that way when nobody else does?' But I kept saying, 'There *are* others. We *do* exist. There *are* people who believe that blowing other people's heads off is a dumb idea. I'm not the only one on earth who thinks as I do.' "

But what if a new kind of society doesn't come into being? What if the revolution never comes?

"Well," Joan says, "I want to have lived my life in such a way that I won't regret any of the things I've done. So even if we never reach the goal, I'll at least have attempted to live a decent life all the way through. I'll have kept on trying to reach people, trying to keep myself open so that *I* can be reached, trying to be kind, trying to learn about love. In my most down moments, I think maybe that will be the most we'll be able to do—to live a life of *trying* to do those things. And if it comes to that, it will, after all, have been quite a lot to have done."

Joan tries to make her principles part of her life in more than conversation. When, for instance, she was one of the stars traveling the country in 1975 as part of Bob Dylan's Rolling Thunder Revue, she was angry when she found out that the bus drivers, the crew, and the security personnel ate at separate places and at separate hours from the performers. *"That,"* she told me, "is segregation. And it's going to stop."

"What if you can't get it to stop?" I asked her.

"Then a lot of us performers," she said, "will go eat with the security people, the bus drivers, and the crew. There are a lot of possible approaches to this kind of problem."

During the tour, there was an internal Rolling Thunder Revue newspaper, and in it Joan wrote one day:

"We strongly suggest that the security people, the bus drivers, and the crew be treated more like human beings and less like bastard children because without them one of the principals [the performers] might be left dead in the wake of the Rolling Thunder Revue."

"Did your Emancipation Proclamation work?" I asked Joan.

"Well, things came together a bit after that. A lot of people, each in his or her own way, began committing small acts of civil disobedience—like taking the bus driver to their table. So the tone has changed and the segregation has lessened."

Joan also works to try to end large-scale injustice far from home. During the 1960s and early 1970s, she had been one of the nation's leading opponents of the war in Vietnam, urging tax resistance, helping to block induction centers, and supporting draft resisters. She believed that American involvement in Vietnam was murderously unjust. And Joan traveled to North Vietnam during the war. At one point she was caught in an air raid conducted by American bombers, because after all, she was in enemy territory—except that she refused to consider the North Vietnamese and the Vietcong in the South to be her enemies.

Joan was in Hanoi during Christmas, 1972, when for the first time during the war in Vietnam, the United States used B-52 bombers against the North Vietnamese. According to a military officer in Guam who was quoted by *The New York*

Times, these military raids were "the biggest aerial operation in the history of warfare."

When she came back home, Joan, during an interview with Tim Cahill of *Rolling Stone,* played a tape that had been made on that Christmas eve in the lobby of Hoa Binh (Peace) Hotel in Hanoi.

As described by Cahill, "Joan Baez starts to sing 'The Lord's Prayer' in her familiar, soaring voice. Suddenly there is an immense concussion, the unmistakable sound of a bomb. The guitar falters, then Joan's voice comes back strong and brave. . . . An air-raid siren screams nearby, cutting directly into the verse about forgiving trespasses. . . .

" 'Get your helmets,' a Vietnamese calls in English. The tape ends with the sounds of confusion: running, scuffling feet and the howl of the air-raid siren."

Joan was under the American bombs for twelve days, and among the horrors and tragedies she saw was a woman, in shock and agony, chanting the same thing over and over as she sifted through the rubble, dazedly picking up bricks and putting them down. Joan asked an interpreter what the woman was chanting. He told her it was an old folk song which asked, "Where are you now, my sons? Where are you now?"

Both her young sons were buried in the rubble.

In a hospital devastated by the bombs, Joan saw a row of corpses—"my first exposure to a line of dead bodies."

She brought back photographs as well as memories. One of them, as Tim Cahill wrote in *Rolling Stone,* "showed a lovely Vietnamese girl of about 17. She was sitting on a high stoop and her legs hung free and bare under a knee-length skirt. Where her feet should have been there was nothing. Her legs ended in blackened stumps at midcalf. 'This girl told me [said Joan] that she lost her legs a week before her wedding. She didn't think that her husband would want her, but he carried her to the wedding on his back.' "

There were four or five bombing raids every night Joan

was in Hanoi, and every time she heard the sirens, Joan and those with her went to the air-raid shelters. During the last raid while she was in Hanoi, Cahill writes, Joan "chose not to huddle in the shelter. Instead she stood on the balcony of her hotel and sang."

I asked her once about the danger she has often been in as a witness against violence.

"Well," she said, "if I started worrying about getting killed for saying the things I say or going to the places I go to, I'd quit doing most of everything I do. There are a million places and times when it could happen, but I just have to forget about them.

"Let me make it clear, though," Joan emphasized, "that I'm by no means looking for martyrdom. There are things worth dying for, but there's a hell of a lot more to *live* for."

11

"Repression is repression.
A rubber hose is a rubber hose.
The beating must feel the same whether a Socialist
or an imperialist is doing it."

In 1979, Joan, who for so long had been one of the more visible opponents of America's huge involvement in the war in Vietnam, shocked and outraged a good many of the antiwar Americans who had marched and protested along with her until America left Vietnam. Joan Baez publicly accused the victorious revolutionary government of Vietnam of being cruelly unjust to large numbers of its citizens. It was punishing and jailing them, she said because they did not hold the proper orthodox views about the new government.

Many Americans who had been alongside Joan in the peace movement felt strongly that no American had the right to criticize anything about the new government of Vietnam after all the bombs that had been dropped on that country by American planes and all the lives destroyed by those bombs. As one British journalist, John Pilger, was writing at the time, "thousands of children in Hanoi and Haiphong alone . . . are permanently deaf as the result of the [American] bombing at Christmas, 1972."

To criticize the government of this shattered country, said some American peace activists, was to "betray" the Vietnamese.

"Which Vietnamese?" Joan answered. For there were new victims in Vietnam. This time they were not victims of America but rather of their own government. To be silent about what was happening would be a betrayal of *these* Vietnamese.

For example, a woman in Ho Chi Minh City (formerly Saigon) told a reporter for the French newspaper, *Le Nouvel Observateur:* "The police came at dawn. They took my husband away, saying he would return quickly, so quickly that it wasn't worth the trouble to pack a valise. That was seven months ago. I've had no news of him. I've knocked at all the doors. Nothing."

That was in the fall of 1978. The year before, eight Vietnamese signed their names to a "Manifesto on Human Rights" —a protest against the imprisonment of Vietnamese who had committed the "crime" of not being enthusiastic enough about the new government. Some indeed were critical of the new government but had done nothing to try to overthrow or otherwise subvert it. Others of the new prisoners had worked for the previous, American-supported governments, and so were held under suspicion by the new regime. But also imprisoned were Vietnamese who had fought against the previous American-supported governments.

These prisoners were detained in what were called "reeducation camps." Herded into them were writers, pacifists, Buddhists, Catholics, trade union and women's group leaders, lawyers, scholars, musicians, painters. Some of the prisoners were made to suffer horribly, particularly those who were shoved into small Connex boxes—metal or wood shipping containers left over from the war in Vietnam. As days went by and the sun made the temperature inside the boxes rise higher and higher, prisoners died.

When Joan Baez found out about these reeducation camps, she wrote an "Open Letter to the Socialist Republic of Vietnam" and sent copies throughout the American peace movement in order to gather signatures. Later, she paid with her own money for the printing of the letter as an ad in *The New York Times*, *The Washington Post*, the *San Francisco Chronicle*, and the *Los Angeles Times*. Also receiving copies of the letter were the President of the Socialist Republic of Vietnam and the secretary general of the United Nations. I was one of those who signed the letter.

Joan was denounced by many in the peace movement who either could not bring themselves to believe that this repression was taking place under the "revolutionary" government or who insisted, as one of them put it, that "We do not have the moral right to condemn anything done by the government of Vietnam."

To which Joan Baez said, "As in the sixties, we raised our voices so that the people of Vietnam may live, so now some of us are raising our voices so that the people in Vietnam may live."

"But if you're wrong?" Joan kept being asked. "What if you're exaggerating the conditions in Vietnam?"

Said Joan, "I would rather err in unintentionally offending government officials anywhere in the world (to whom I would happily apologize later if I have been mistaken) than offend one political prisoner whom I might now conceivably help and whom later I may never be able to reach."

But she was not wrong. As Amnesty International—the most respected of all human rights organizations—eventually reported, the reeducation camps in Vietnam were as Joan had described them, and worse.

But did Joan's open letter and her newspaper ads have any effect? Ginetta Sagan, one of the most experienced human rights activists in the world, and a longtime worker with Amnesty International, told me that because of Joan Baez, several thousand prisoners were freed from Vietnam's reeducation camps. The government of that country did not like being publicly accused by this woman—who had been an honored, endangered guest during the early 1970s—of being similar to the government it had overthrown.

The camps still exist, and Amnesty International continues to work for the liberation of these prisoners of conscience. And Joan continues to be involved in making human rights a reality in Vietnam and in other countries as well.

Joan has participated in Amnesty International projects, and she has also set up her own organization, Humanitas International Human Rights Committee.

In 1981, she and a co-worker, Jeanne Murphy, traveled for five weeks to Mexico, Argentina, Chile, Brazil, and Nicaragua. In the newsletter of her Humanitas International, Joan reported on what they had found. In Argentina, where the military dictatorship was then still in power, Joan met with some of the mothers of the *desaparecidos* (the disappeared). More than fifteen thousand people had vanished after having been taken into custody by security forces. Some of the mothers eventually discovered their loved ones had been murdered, after having been tortured and maimed almost beyond recognition.

One woman, now living in Mexico, spoke to Joan of the murders in Argentina of her husband, three of her children, and other members of her family between 1975 and 1978:

"On December 24, 1975, my daughter, Noni, who was twenty-four years old at the time, was kidnapped in an army jeep, at ten o'clock, in the villa where she was a literacy teacher. I looked for her, spoke to a lot of people, but only on January 8, 1976, in the Courthouse Number Eight of La Plata, did they tell me my daughter had died. And as proof they offered me a jar—number twenty-eight—with Noni's hands in it as identification."

Another mother of a *desaparecido* told another woman, "You are lucky because you *know* your child is dead."

A woman who did not know whether her child was dead or alive told Joan:

"I can't think that my daughter is not alive. If I do, then I

have to admit that she's been killed in cold blood. And that I
resist. But at night, especially on stormy nights, after saying
good-bye to her picture, my mind is a parade of images. . . .
Did she suffer? Did they torture her? Was she abused? Where is
she? . . . It is a parade of images of things that go and come,
and it is very difficult to accept all of that."

"One feels a lot of diminished self-importance," Joan said,
"when you're with the mothers of the disappeared."

While Joan was in Argentina, she was followed twenty-
four hours a day by two carloads of security police and was not
allowed by the government to perform even a free concert.

In Chile, where poets and singers are killed and books are
burned by the government, Joan was able to arrange a free
concert in a church, which was surrounded by armed police.
Thousands of young Chileans came to hear her, shouting,
"Freedom!" "Freedom!" "Justice!" as Joan came on stage. But
commercial concerts were forbidden. In Chile too there were
mothers of the disappeared, and Joan stood with them as they
all sang "We Shall Overcome."

In Brazil, Joan committed an act of nonviolent civil disobedience immediately after the government canceled all her concerts and said she could not perform anywhere in that country.
Joan went to Federal Police Headquarters in São Paulo, and, in
front of the building, sang with her customary force and clarity.

On another occasion in Brazil, before the government
banned all her appearances, a concert was suddenly cancelled
by the Office of Censorship shortly before it was to have begun.
The hall was crowded with expectant listeners, but Joan was
told by friends that if she defied the order and sang from the
stage, everybody in the hall—not only Joan—would be in jeop-
ardy.

After half an hour, Joan went out into the audience and sat
down. Spontaneously, everybody began to sing, Joan among
them. The police took no action.

As for Nicaragua, thinking back on what she had seen there, Joan wrote in *Humanitas International:*

The men and women we met [the revolutionaries, the Sandinistas], who had unequivocally put their lives on the line for the liberation of Nicaragua, were highly admirable human beings.

I do not fault them for their bravery or for taking the only seemingly available route [violent rebellion] to throw off their oppressors.

And yet, there is still something that troubles me: what I dislike and fear is the sight of ten-year-old kids marching around with M-16s slung over their shoulders, identifying with those weapons of death. I have concerns that they will have great difficulty in moving away from the posture of militarism and the false sense of power which accompanies it. How easy will it be to take away those weapons and those berets . . . from those kids and create the society that the Sandinistas were talking about in the first place?

What's the alternative to the use of violence to get rid of barbaric governments, like the right-wing Somoza dictatorship in Nicaragua that was overthrown by the Sandinistas?

"We have seen," Joan said, "certain people emerge from the stranglehold of oppression, forcing themselves to be seen and heard in the struggle to create social change *without* the use of arms and violence. People like Lech Walesa in Poland, Mairead Corrigan in Ireland, Danilo Dolci in Italy, Lula [a labor leader] in Brazil, Cesar Chavez and Martin Luther King in the U.S., and, of course, Gandhi in India.

But in the majority of countries, Joan went on, violence is still seen as the only available way to bring an end to oppression. Part of the reason for that, she emphasized, is that people who believe in nonviolence have not done enough reaching out to the oppressed to show them that there *are* specific nonviolent ways by which they can fight for their freedom—as shown, for example, by Martin Luther King and Gandhi.

So Joan Baez has given herself another lifelong assignment: to spread the word about nonviolent alternatives wherever she goes. Including her travels at home.

In 1981, for one example, when the Ku Klux Klan scheduled a rally in San Jose, California, Joan helped organize and then sang at an anti-Klan rally held in a different part of town. Without the counterrally, there might have been a violent confrontation at the Klan meeting. The Baez way enabled people who despise the Klan to say so at a big gathering of their own, thereby avoiding head-breaking on both sides.

During these years, Joan has also continued campaigning for nuclear disarmament, for the release of political prisoners in Russia, and for attention to be paid to the Vietnamese boat people, Cambodian refugees, and others of the homeless.

But as these journeys have continued, what has happened to her singing career? Although she continued to attract large audiences, including many of the young, in Europe, where she also recorded a number of albums, her musical fortunes in the United States were uneven. Record companies were not interested in Joan because her sound and her material were not, they felt, for the mass market. When she toured in this country, however, she attracted sizeable, enthusiastic audiences of her admirers from the 1960s. They remembered her; they wanted more of her.

In the United States, too, young people were coming to her concerts, though not as many as she would have liked. And in all her appearances, she kept doing what she had been doing for twenty-five years: "My job, as I tell my audiences, is to spend half the evening trying to get them to forget the sadnesses of the world, and to spend the other half getting them to remember. It's a tricky business."

By the mid 1980s, Joan saw in the new generation a new

beginning for attention to human rights everywhere, including everyone's right not to die in a nuclear holocaust. At a conference in San Francisco, *Beyond the Blocs: Linking East and West for Disarmament and Human Rights*, she said:

"I was moved to tears hearing students who are suddenly feeling again that maybe it's possible for people to get together and actually do something. It may be the younger generation is getting tired of being called the 'me' generation, the generation that doesn't think."

On July 4, 1985, the music concert with the largest audience in the history of the world was held for a new generation, whose presence at the event was a sign that its members cared for more than themselves. The Live Aid concert for African Famine Relief, broadcast around the world from JFK Stadium in Philadelphia and Wembley Stadium in London, lasted sixteen hours, raised forty million dollars, and reached one and a half billion people in one hundred sixty countries.

Opening the American section of the concert was Joan Baez.

All day and into the night, the most renowned of the rockers came on stage—Mick Jagger, Tina Turner, Bob Dylan, Lionel Richie, Elton John, Paul McCartney, David Bowie, Phil Collins, Madonna, Queen, and many more. Musicians from Austria, the Netherlands, West Germany, Yugoslavia, Japan, Australia, and the Soviet Union were beamed by satellites to the giant screens in New York and London. Among them was Autograph, the first rock band in the Soviet Union to be seen live on television.

At the exhilarating end of it all, singing and moving on stage with the other superstars was, again, Joan Baez. The "solo grace" of her presence that day, said *The Washington Post*, "was an obvious bridge between 60s political consciousness and commitment—and the new wave of the 80s."

A couple of weeks later, during a radio interview in New

York, Joan was still riding a natural high from the Live Aid concert but was also thoughtful.

"We're in a time," she said, "where, on the one hand, it's like staring at a tidal wave coming at you. This wild short-sighted optimism: let's make a lot of money; let's all watch MTV.

"On the other hand, there are those other things that are more meaningful, but take so much time and patience. For instance, I know that in my lifetime, I'm not going to see the end of hunger, the end of apathy, the end of the military nation-state. None of this gets done in a spring vacation. Knowing that, you don't get disappointed, but you do get frustrated. And that's why you have to stay active. Otherwise, you'd go under.

"By staying active, you have little victories and big defeats. But it's the little victories that count."

And it's being consistent over all these years that also counts. In *The Village Voice*, in the 1970s, Marlene Nadle wrote, "Baez's refusal to swing with the fashions has given her an integrity and authority few pop idols, musical or political, can match."

Nadle quoted a young woman at a concert by Joan: "Baez may not be fashionable or hip. But she's discovered the secret. She always knows who she's coming as."

Joan herself talks of her consistency as being rooted in "nonviolence and fairness. It works through what we at Humanitas call 'Seeing Through Both Eyes.'

"To be consistent, for one example, you have to be able to see repression in left-wing countries and in right-wing countries and in Third World countries. Repression is repression. A rubber hose is a rubber hose. The beating must feel about the same whether a Socialist or an imperialist is doing it."

And what makes it worth spending so much of your life trying to get governments to be human?

"It's not that it's the moral thing to do," says Joan, "or the proper thing to do. It's the only deeply joyous thing to do. It has its pain, but the rewards are so immense!"

And the funny things in life also keep her going. When asked about the attempts, some of them by wives of United States Senators, to control rock lyrics, Joan said, "As for putting the words of the songs on the albums, I think that's wonderful. Young people would read again."

V

ADAH MAURER: ENDING VIOLENCE AGAINST THE NEXT GENERATION IN AMERICA

12

*"We should join the majority of civilized nations
in banning corporal punishment altogether
from American schools."*

The boy, an eighth-grader, had been hospitalized for two days
after a beating in school by his teacher. He had been struck
repeatedly. His crime: talking in class when he hadn't been
asked to.

The boy's mother wanted to file a complaint of assault
against the teacher, but the district attorney's office talked her
out of it. Corporal punishment by a teacher is lawful in the
state, the mother was told, and all the teacher would have to
tell the jury is that he was disciplining the student in good
faith.

I talked to the mother, who didn't want her name used for
fear that reprisals would be taken against her son in the school.
"The man who hit my boy," she told me, "should be abandoned from children. Why, he took another boy and slammed
him into the locker. I cannot understand how they let people
like this teach children. It's like letting people from a crazy
institution take over a school, throw children against the wall,
beat them with boat paddles, and they say they're teaching
them.

"When my boy was in the fifth grade," the angry woman
continued, "he got up out of his seat. That's all he did. They
tied him to a chair with a rope. Then, when they started hitting

him, I told that sorry devil of a principal, 'I don't want anyone every laying a hand on my child again.' He told me to shut my mouth.

"My child has been abused," the mother continued. "And not only him. Good lord, not only him. But you cannot whip a child and make him learn anything. I do believe that if you give a child some love, even a little love, and let him know you care for him, he'll learn."

I asked the woman if she had given up on trying to stop the beating of children in the schools in that city in Arkansas.

"No," she said. "I'm working in the PTA here. I'm trying to convince parents to sit in at the school board meetings and tell the members of the board what's going on in the classrooms. Expose the hitters. Keep pointing at them. And insist on getting more counselors so that kids needing help will get help—not a beating. What a child needs is confidence in grown-ups, not to fear them."

In England, in 1669, "a lively boy," as he was described at the time, presented a petition to the Speaker of the House of Commons. The boy was acting for young people throughout the land who were being beaten as part of their lessons in school.

We the children of the land, the petition said, implore an end to corporal punishment in the schools. Teachers and the heads of schools, the children's petition went on, should no longer have the power to terrorize students. A schoolmaster who can only maintain order with violence is "no more fit for that function than if he had no skill in Latin and Greek."

The Children's Petition of 1669 never came to a vote in Parliament. In 1698, the children of England tried again, urging Parliament to pass "an Act to remedy the foule abuse of children at schools." This time the petition included accounts of specific cruel punishments—"such stories," said the petition, "that would make a heart of stone bleed."

Not only boys were abused, the children charged, but girls too were whipped. "Only Parliament," the children of England cried, "can deliver the nation from this evil."

As in 1669, so again nearly thirty years later, as British historian C. B. Freeman reports, the children's plea was ignored by Parliament. And students kept being beaten in school, until corporal punishment was finally abolished in England as of 1987.

Other countries, however, stopped corporal punishment in their schools much, much earlier—Poland (1783), the Netherlands (1820), Belgium (1867), Austria (1870), France (1881), Finland (1890), Sweden (1958), Denmark (1967). Indeed, nearly all European countries, including the Soviet Union and all the other Communist bloc countries, have by now abolished corporal punishment. In 1970, Bavaria became the last state in West Germany to stop the beating of schoolchildren; Ireland abandoned this "foule abuse" of children in 1982. But in the United States and South Africa, corporal punishment is still the primitive rule.

Only nine of our states have outlawed this form of legal child abuse: Massachusetts, New Jersey, Hawaii, Maine, New York, Rhode Island, New Hampshire, Vermont, and most recently, California. A growing number of cities and some towns have also instructed school officials to throw their sticks and bats away, but elsewhere in the United States the beat goes on.

And what are kids being hit with?

Testifying before the Senate Subcommittee on Juvenile Justice in October, 1984, Dr. Irwin Hyman of Temple University's National Center for the Study of Corporal Punishment said:

"In some districts, the administration issues 'regulation' instruments to be utilized by its staff . . . paddles, leather straps, or a 'thin rattan.' . . . Some [educators] have wrapped the paddles with masking tape; others have had holes drilled in the paddle so that air would not be able to 'work as a cushion' [and ease the pain]. One case even involved the teacher's name being drilled across the paddle."

That personalized paddle reminded me of a conversation I had with a group of public school kids in Dallas. They told me of a principal whose first name was Elmer. Painted on the paddle he used on wrongdoers was ELMER THE TERRIBLE.

One student said, "He's got that paddle with him all the time. Last week he even showed up in the playground with it. You're supposed to be able to make some noise in the playground! My cousin, he's scared to go to school. He ain't been hit yet, but he figures that sooner or later Elmer the Terrible is going to get him."

In his Senate testimony, Dr. Irwin Hyman, who also appeared on behalf of the American Psychological Association, told the senators of the many other kinds of weapons that teachers and administrators use against children:

> . . . hands, fists, rulers and yardsticks, "doubled-over" belts, lacrosse and broom sticks, baseball bats, large slabs of wood, and metal or steel pipes. Some children have reportedly been disciplined with a metal cattle prod and an electrostatic generator.
>
> In addition, there are news accounts of children being subjected to the cutting off of their hair; being put in a storeroom, box, cloakroom, and/or school vault; thrown against a wall, desk, and/or concrete pillar; forced to run the "gauntlet" or "belt line"; forced to perform punishment push-ups; disrobed in private or before peers; made to stand on their toes for long periods of time; punched, dragged by the arm and/or hair; had meals withheld; choked; forced to lie on a wet floor in their clothing; forced to eat cigarettes; and tied to a chair with rope.

Are there any serious injuries?

Said Dr. Hyman, whose center at Temple University is the nation's leading research source on corporal punishment in the schools:

Many believe that corporal punishment only leaves transient bruises which last for a few hours . . . [one] child [however] was hospitalized with head injuries for ten days. Other children have . . . required treatment for skin and muscle injuries, emergency surgery for a rupture due to an injury to the testicles, and [others] have sustained possible permanent damage to the buttocks and legs . . .

Some children have sustained headaches or dizziness from being hit on the head, or a cerebral concussion and sprained neck; [others are] left with impaired hearing after being thrown against a wall and struck, [some have] sustained a sprained arm and facial abrasions when the child's arm was twisted behind her back and she was wrestled to the ground. [Other students] had a bloody or fractured nose, had a two-inch patch of hair pulled out of the scalp, suffered a gash in the eye that required seven stitches and a possible hairline fracture of the bones beneath the eye. An eighth-grade boy had two teeth chipped and had the ligaments in his mouth torn when his teacher struck him in the mouth with his lunch bag, which contained a twelve-ounce bottle of soda.

The beat goes on and on.

An arthritic and rheumatic third-grade boy was spanked [with a wooden drawer divider] even after the parent indicated that she did not want her child spanked. Due to the stress of being spanked, a seven-year-old had an epileptic seizure—the first convulsion she had had in over a year. An asthmatic ten-year-old girl was struck across the chest because she mispronounced a word during reading class. A boy with muscular dystrophy was treated for abrasions and contusions after being hit about the left and right knees and thighs with a ruler.

And this, Dr. Hyman emphasizes, is just the tip of the iceberg of cruelty in this nation's schools.

The cruelest punishment of a child in school that I know

of took place in a small Texas town. The father of the boy told
me what had happened. His son, ten, was dying of a blood
disease. His parents decided that so long as the boy had some
strength, they would keep sending him to school so that he
could be with his friends.

The parents told school officials that their son was dying,
but nonetheless, because the child sometimes talked in class
when he wasn't supposed to, he was beaten, and beaten hard,
by his teacher.

"I have given up trying to understand how people could
do that," his father told me. We first met a few months after the
boy had died of the blood disease. "To think that people who
say they're educators can beat a child they know is dying. They
have a sickness that is beyond me. But what still makes me
furious is that there wasn't a thing I could do about it. The
principal and the teachers told me they had the right to beat
my boy. And there it was, right in the law!"

Every year in American public schools, according to the
National Center for the Study of Corporal Punishment, there
are at least two or three million incidents of corporal punishment. Most, to be sure, do not inflict lasting injury; but as
we've seen, a considerable number of the assaults do cause both
physical and emotional damage. As Jimmy Dunne, executive
director of P.O.P.S. (People Opposed to Paddling of Students,
Inc.) in Houston, Texas, says, "In any other setting outside of
our schools, hitting another person would be a criminal act.
And hitting another person with a board is clearly assault. . . .

"Subjecting a child to this sort of treatment is humiliating
and diminishes his or her mental health. It teaches that hitting
is the way to solve problems. This adds to the violence in our
society. . . . Children grow up treating others the way they
are treated. We must do a better job with the next generation.
Corporal punishment is legalized child abuse."

Even a cop can't prevent his child from being assaulted in
a school if he lives in a city or state where corporal punishment

is legal. Consider the case of a third-grader in Rochester, New York. He is the son of a sergeant in the Monroe County Sheriff's Office. In school one morning, the youngster had been kicked by another boy and without meaning to break the concentration of his fellow students, he yelled out in pain. A rule of that public school was *no noisemaking in class.* So the principal whacked the boy twelve times on the buttocks with a heavy wooden paddle.

Later that day, the boy, again without meaning any harm, tripped over a desk in class. In falling, he again made some noise, and once more the principal bashed him with his wooden paddle. When the child came home, his father later told me, "You could see raw flesh showing blood."

Friends of the father in the police department made color pictures of the wounds for use in court, and the father sent me a set of the prints. It was clear that a prison guard responsible for inflicting that kind of injury on a prisoner would have been fired and probably jailed as well.

The father sued the school principal for assault, but the case was thrown out of court. A New York State law said that public school educators could lawfully administer corporal punishment short of "deadly force." The boy was still alive, so the principal had not broken the law.

The father was furious and bewildered. He said to me, "I just don't understand how they can keep this corporal punishment law on the books. In my job, I don't have the right to beat prisoners, even though some of them are real sickies. And I *shouldn't* have that right.

"Not only can't I beat adult prisoners, but if I were working in a state institution for juvenile delinquents, I would be breaking the law if I beat any of them, either."

As of 1985, however, neither the sergeant's son nor any other public school student in the state of New York can any longer be beaten in school. The Board of Regents, which supervises all schooling in the state, has finally ended corporal punishment throughout New York State.

One of the causes of that decision is the work of a vigorous, determined, white-haired woman, Adah Maurer, who lives in Berkeley, California. For years, she has devoted practically all of her time to outlawing corporal punishment. A number of those, for example, who helped shape the New York State Board of Regents' decision to end kid whacking were readers of Adah Maurer's quarterly publication, *The Last ? Resort.* It's the newsletter of her organization, End Violence Against the Next Generation, Inc., and is the only publication dealing exclusively with corporal punishment in the schools.

Each issue tells of students around the country—from kindergarten through high school—who have been cruelly beaten. Adah Maurer also covers court cases brought by indignant students and their parents, she reports on cities and towns that have been persuaded to end corporal punishment, and she prints testimony before legislatures by psychiatrists and educators on the enduring harm that can be caused by beating schoolchildren.

Stories from Adah Maurer's newsletter have been quoted in articles in mass-circulation magazines, and they've been used by parents in various towns and cities who are trying to get corporal punishment abolished. Slowly, steadily, through the years, Adah has had a lot to do with the fact that an increasing number of school districts around the country have done away with corporal punishment. Although the Supreme Court had ruled in 1977 (*Ingraham* v. *Wright*) that corporal punishment is not unconstitutional under the "cruel and unusual punishment" clause of the Eighth Amendment to the Constitution, Adah knew it could nonetheless be outlawed state by state and city by city, if one worked hard enough. The courts are not the only way to get rid of a harmful practice. Local legislatures and school boards can do it too.

In June 1985, three of the most influential groups in the country—The Parent Teachers Association, the American Medical Association, and the American Bar Association—all came out with strong condemnations of corporal punishment in the schools. In various ways, the spirit of Adah Maurer and her extensive research on this form of legal child beating helped create the momentum that led to the passage of those resolutions by the three organizations.

The American Medical Association, like all the groups that have come out against corporal punishment, noted that a teacher or school administrator could still use force to defend himself or herself from attack, to disarm a student with a knife or some other weapon, to protect other individuals from violence directed against them, and to protect school or personal property.

Pointing out that a 1984 survey revealed that corporal punishment is widely used "with students at every grade level in virtually all regions of the country," the doctors' group cited the conclusion of the National Education Association that "the use of physical punishment inclines everyone in the school community to regard students as less than human and the schools as dehumanizing."

In *its* condemnation of corporal punishment, the American Bar Association said flat out that beating kids in school is "a form of child abuse that is contrary to current knowledge of human behavior and sound educational practices." As an example, the lawyers cited what had happened in West Virginia when a teacher, "without apparent provocation . . . struck a sixth-grade student with a paddle made of hard thick rubber about five inches in width, violently shoved the child against a large stationary desk, and then struck her repeatedly and violently. As a result, the child was taken to a nearby hospital where she remained for ten days, suffering possible permanent injuries."

Moreover, said the nation's leading organization of lawyers, the American Bar Association, corporal punishment is defined not only as inflicting pain by striking a child with a stick, hand, or some other instrument. Corporal punishment also means inflicting "unnecessary excessive discomfort, such as forced standing for an excessively long period of time, confinement in an uncomfortable space, or forcing children to eat obnoxious substances."

The ABA too quoted from a report on corporal punishment by the National Education Association, the nation's largest teachers' union:

"Corporal punishment is used much more often against pupils who are smaller and weaker than the teacher; it is used more frequently against poor children and members of minority groups than against children of white, middle-class families.

"In many cases, corporal punishment causes lasting psychological damage to children."

During the debate on the resolution at the annual meeting of the American Bar Association, one delegate said that if a parent inflicted the kind of abuse on a child that some school personnel do when *they* hit children, a court would take the child away from that parent.

"We should join the majority of civilized nations," said the delegate, "in banning corporal punishment altogether."

13

("The principal kept three sizes of paddles on hand . . .
The heavy wooden paddle that he called 'Mister Charley'
was reserved strictly for the backsides
of boys from the slums.
The middle-sized Ping-Pong paddle
was used on middle-class kids.
And 'Popsicle Pete,' which was nothing
more than a tongue depressor a physician might use,
was reserved for the children of the affluent.")

As the one individual most responsible for the awakening of more and more Americans to the fact that corporal punishment is child abuse, Adah Maurer keeps looking ahead to all the states and cities and towns from which child beating in the schools must *still* be banished. And so she keeps reporting in her newsletter, *The Last ? Resort*, about new documented horror stories, new allies in various parts of the country fighting against corporal punishment, and new cities that have decided to become civilized.

This is the kind of information that has appeared through the years in *The Last ? Resort:* Nancy Berla, who directs a hotline for children abused in school on behalf of the National Committee for Citizens in Education, reports that "In many schools teachers carry their paddles attached to their belts. The teachers are accustomed to using the paddle on children for petty or trivial behavior, such as being late to class, not having the right color pencil, missing the school bus to go home, talking at lunchtime, or being out of their seats without permission."

She adds that "in cases where the paddling is severe enough to cause bruises or other injuries, parents often report to child abuse authorities, intending to place charges against the teacher or principal who inflicted the paddling. They soon learn that such incidents are not legally considered child abuse and cannot be investigated or acted upon by the agency. The parents may appeal to the school board, charging cruel and excessive punishment. But the school board members [in places where corporal punishment has not yet been outlawed] invariably back the teacher and the principal, and are not responsive to the parents' objections to this type of punishment. . . ."

What has made Adah Maurer's magazine so useful and influential around the country is that it gives specific facts about specific places, and then Adah puts the writer of the facts in touch with other people in his or her city or state who are also working to end adult violence against schoolchildren.

Adah, for instance, reprinted an article by Ohio psychologist Dr. Robert Fatham from the December, 1983 bulletin of the Ohio Psychological Association. He noted that "Children's Hospital in Columbus recorded twenty-eight cases of child abuse by teachers in just one year. There is no way of knowing how many cases were seen by other hospitals, physicians, or were never taken for medical care.

"Columbus public schools, with just over 60,000 pupils, report over 20,000 cases of corporal punishment during the last school year. *Most school systems don't tabulate these incidents.* It's not required by law nor by the rule of the State Board of Education.

"*Schools are the only institutions in American society where legal sanction is given for one person to hit another,* and it is used many times for the most trivial of reasons. In the Marysville Schools, for example, five first-graders were lined up in the hall and hit three times each with a board: two had forgotten to put their names on the paper [they were working on]; one circled words on a reading list instead of underlining them; and the other two had made similar mistakes. One of these children was my six-year-old daughter. Protests to the principal, superintendent and school board were fruitless." (Emphasis added.)

Dr. Fatham decided to do something about this kind of official abuse. He contacted a number of organizations in Ohio to form the Committee for More Effective School Discipline. And Adah Maurer, using her contacts, enabled various anti–corporal punishment people in Ohio to get in touch with Dr. Fatham and each other.

Their goal, of course, is to expel corporal punishment from every public school in Ohio. They will eventually succeed because they're well organized and they keep collecting hard evidence of this kind of child abuse by teachers and principals. The state legislature has already acknowledged their growing force by allowing at least local option in Ohio. That is, from now on, if a city or town does not want its children beaten in school, they have the power to get rid of corporal punishment. Child beating in the schools is no longer automatically state-wide.

The Ohio campaign, like many others aimed at banishing corporal punishment, made good use of Adah Maurer's master list of humane human beings. She keeps adding to that list by subscribing to a clipping service that sends her items from all over the country that have to do with corporal punishment.

"I get my names," Adah Maurer says, "from many of those clippings. It may be someone trying to get a school board to do something about a teacher who keeps on hitting kids. It may be someone who wrote an angry letter to the editor about corporal punishment, or someone involved in a court case concerning a student hurt while being physically punished. When there is an address attached to the name, I write him or her a letter.

"I congratulate them for taking a stand on corporal punishment, and I tell them they're not alone. I send a copy of our brochures from End Violence Against the Next Generation, and I ask, 'How can we help?'

"It's important to these people," Adah emphasizes, "that they hear from the outside world. Usually they're being denounced where they are, and getting an encouraging word is like manna from heaven. This encouragement becomes all the more important if the battle is taking place in a small town, where the ones who want to stop corporal punishment are likely to be surrounded by seas of ignorance when it comes to whether children should be hit."

How did Adah Maurer become involved in this battle, which has taken over much of her life? It started at a time when, as a school psychologist, she herself was surrounded by a sea of ignorance.

Adah's first experience with a community devoted to corporal punishment in its schools came in 1962. She had come to Northern California from Chicago, where she herself had been educated and had later worked in the public schools as a teacher of gym, geometry, typing, history, and English. She had also earned a Master of Arts in educational psychology from the University of Chicago. During all those years Adah was a student and a teacher in Chicago, corporal punishment was not used in that city's schools. And in raising her own daughter and son, Adah never inflicted any physical punishment on them.

But then came Shasta County in California. Adah had gotten a job as a school psychologist in 1962 in the town of Redding up in the lumber country of Shasta County. Many of the mountain people there were second generation Okies—the children of poor farmers who had come west from Oklahoma and surrounding states during the Great Depression of the 1930s. They were fiercely independent and did not take kindly to outsiders interfering with their way of life.

Adah Maurer has written, for this book, a memoir of her time in Shasta County:

> One day a pleasant young teacher stopped me as I was getting into my car to ask me about a child who worried her. I listened while she described a very troubled child. And then she said, "I hardly ever spank him anymore unless he crawls under the piano."
>
> Startled, I said, "You what?"
>
> She repeated the sentence a bit uncertainly, then added, "Is that wrong?"
>
> I was still dumbfounded. "You spank him? Whatever for?"
>
> This led to a description of her co-worker, the teacher of grades one and two in the two-room schoolhouse, who spanked every child every day. I had to believe her; she was obviously sincere.

But this was only the beginning of Adah Maurer's education in official child beating. She continues:

> In one small community in a foothill town, population between two and three hundred, an eleven-year-old had become the unpaid town prostitute. I didn't know that when I first met her. In school she sat numb and silent and was paddled for being inattentive. When she no longer cried from the beatings, they referred her to me, but I hadn't a clue to the cause of her silence. A phone call from the Fundamentalist minister who served her church hinted at dark doings.
>
> I asked, "You mean you're afraid she may fall into sinful ways with boys?"
>
> He said, "She already has."
>
> "With whom?"
>
> "Oh, everybody: her brothers first and her father and her uncles, and then even strangers."
>
> I talked this over with the young woman probation officer. She said, "Leave it to me." She scooped up the

child, had her examined, found every venereal disease known to the medical profession, and took custody of the child with the father's agreement. If that hadn't happened, that child would still have been continually abused sexually—and beaten in school because she had trouble keeping her mind on her studies in class.

Then there was a nine-year-old who admittedly had a foul mouth, which he used in a shouting match he got into with his principal, who had been an army officer. The principal took the boy out to a building on the school grounds and beat him so badly that he could not walk home but had to crawl. His mother said, "I thought he had been run over by a car when he came crawling in the front gate."

I testified at a hearing for another boy who was about to be sent to Juvenile Hall for persistent truancy. I told the judge that the boy had an IQ of 60, and that the boy had told me he was late to school each day because his family had no clock (he could not have told time if they did). He was also late because he had to feed and dress his little brothers and sisters because his mother was sick. The judge was furious at the school system for not having done anything about the family and its problems except to paddle this boy because he was late to school.

On a trip to a school located in a town far up in the mountains of Shasta County, Adah Maurer met a Chehalis Indian boy who "told me about his brother who had almost choked when he was dumped head first into a trash can and was beaten on his backside by a teacher while he was in that position."

Back in Redding, she kept trying to persuade the local teachers and principals to put away their paddles. She got nowhere. And so, when a young boy was beaten so badly in school that he had large bruises on his back and legs, Adah wrote an angry letter to the local newspaper.

"I had the curious belief," she recalls, "that when the people of the town read what was going on, they would rise up and rescue their children. Well, there was a furor, but it was directed at me. I was fired and left town on the 5:00 A.M. bus."

She returned to Berkeley, and there, newly aware of how widespread corporal punishment actually is, Adah also discovered that it was no less shocking for being familiar.

One day she heard a principal tell of how he had forced a young boy to confess that he had broken a school rule. The child was literally on his knees begging for mercy. The principal called the boy's mother, who told him, "I know just what that brat is telling you. He's saying you can't hit him, that I won't let you. Well, don't you believe a word of it. You just take it out on his hide."

"And I did," the principal recalled with great satisfaction. "I hit him seven times."

Adah came across another principal who admitted, as *The Berkeley Paper* reported, that "he kept three sizes of paddles on hand. Depending on the social status of the child—not on the severity of the infraction—the principal selected and applied the paddle of his choice.

"The heavy wooden paddle that he called 'Mister Charley' was reserved strictly for the backsides of boys from the slums. The middle-sized Ping-Pong paddle was used on middle-class kids. And 'Popsicle Pete,' which was nothing more than a tongue depressor a physician might use, was reserved for the children of the affluent."

Enough was enough! Adah Maurer began to make plans to abolish corporal punishment. While working as a school psychologist she gave lectures to adult audiences on the barbarism of corporal punishment. Some audiences were receptive; others responded with snickers and laughter. She also sent intensively researched articles on child beating in the schools to professional magazines. But at the time—the early 1970s—they weren't interested in the subject. Neither were such general publications as *Parents Magazine* and *The Parent-Teachers Associa-*

tion Magazine. The letters of rejection said, "This subject matter would not interest our readers."

Years later, I asked Adah why there had been such indifference by both the professional and the general magazines. "Those magazines," she said, "mostly go to people in the metropolitan centers, where corporal punishment is less harsh, if it exists at all, than in small-town and rural areas. Furthermore, the people who get those magazines usually have children who are well behaved and so go through school without getting hit. Accordingly, these people have no direct experience, through their children or in their own school years, with the brutality that a lot of kids, most of them from another class, have to endure.

"Even today, there are people who do not believe the awful things that go on in some schools because *they* don't hear about it."

Despite the indifference and the occasional snickers, Adah Maurer kept writing articles, lecturing, finding allies in various parts of the country, and having a great deal to do with the awakening of the American Psychological Association to the seriousness and extent of the problem. Year after year, she filled the pages of *The Last ? Resort* with case histories and with the small but growing number of victories in the courts, as some teachers and principals were finally fined and sometimes even lost their jobs for assaulting kids.

It looks now, Adah feels, as if legal child abuse may eventually end. It will take quite a while, though. After all, only nine states have outlawed the bashing of kids. (Adah Maurer had a lot to do with the abolition of corporal punishment in 1986, in the ninth—her home state of California.) But more and more cities are forbidding corporal punishment. Among them: Chicago, Washington, New York, Los Angeles, Seattle, San Francisco, Baltimore, Pittsburgh, Atlanta, Salt Lake City, New Orleans, New Haven, Palo Alto, and more. But there are still all those states and cities and towns where this sort of humiliation of a youngster and a family takes place:

In a Texas city, a high school senior with a good academic record, who was working after school so he could pay for his own car, broke a school rule one morning. He parked his car in the wrong place. The punishment was to be three blows with a heavy wooden paddle. He refused to be hit and was suspended for three days. But that wasn't punishment enough. He was told that he would not be readmitted to school, and therefore could not graduate, unless he took those three blows.

In a letter to an administrator of the school, the student's mother wrote:

> I have no quarrel . . . regarding your right to punish my son for violating a rule of parking in the school parking lot. It was a careless act, and he is aware that I am very displeased that he should cause all of us trouble by violating such a simple rule. A three-day suspension seems to me to be adequate punishment for this first violation, but he would accept whatever additional suspension or other punishment you deem proper—short of corporal punishment—and we assure you that this violation will not occur again.
>
> I am morally opposed to corporal punishment. I consider it archaic, barbaric, and counterproductive to all the values I believe parents and teachers should try to promote in their young. It could only serve to degrade and humiliate my son without teaching a lesson of any humane value. In my opinion it would equally degrade the person administering the blows. It is a lesson in might makes right, which I have taught against as long as my son can remember. It may be a small matter to you, but is basic to my deepest beliefs and those I have taught him. . . .
>
> My son has given no one any trouble. He is a gentle person, intelligent, hardworking, and mature for his age. Do you sincerely believe that the best way to deal with young men is by humiliating them?

Perhaps you do not consider him a young man and I will not belabor the point that the draft board disagrees. If you consider him a child, then perhaps you would agree with the laws recently enacted in some states that parents are responsible for the acts of their children. I do not mean to be facetious when I say that, as the one totally responsible for my son's belief—that is, that he has the right to retain some dignity and refuse to be whipped like a slave or animal—I am the proper person to whom you should deliver your blows. I am willing and would receive them without taking the matter any further.

It is, of course, most important to my son, his father, and me that he is able to complete the few short months before graduation. We fully understand that you have it in your power to deny him this important event. I ask that you please consider alternative punishment if the three-day suspension is not sufficient. Surely you do not dislike him this much and if so, may I try to understand why? In any case, I could never give my consent to anything as distasteful and repulsive to me as having you humiliate him by striking him. I find it almost impossible to believe that anyone should seriously believe that such methods of punishment are constructive and helpful in any way.

I ask you to please reconsider.

The school authorities refused to reconsider. And they refused to accept the mother's offer to take the three blows in place of her son.

After days of anguish, the high school senior broke down for the first time and said to his father, "Dad, I want to finish school."

The father and his son went to the school, and the father watched as a school official struck his son three times.

The boy did get his high school diploma. But what else did he learn from this experience?

That might makes right. That education is humiliation.

It is because violations of young people's dignity continue

to take place from elementary school through high school at a rate of two to three million incidents a year that Adah Maurer still devotes practically all of her days to searching out these barbaric practices and trying to end them.

Adah Maurer is a vigorous eighty-one years old, with much yet to do.

Much of the rest of the world, including Israel, the Congo, the Philippines, New Caledonia, Gabon, Tahiti, Qatar, Mexico, and recently, England, have abolished corporal punishment; yet large parts of this nation remain as they were in 1853 when the Indiana Supreme Court declared, "The public seems to cling to the despotism in the government of schools which has been discarded everywhere else. . . . The husband can no longer moderately chastise his wife; nor the master his servant, or his apprentice. Even the degrading cruelties of the naval service have been arrested. Why the person of the schoolboy . . . should be less sacred in the eyes of the law than that of the apprentice or the sailor, is not easily explained."

It is still not easily explained. In the years ahead, the young now attending school will themselves become parents and members of school boards and state legislatures. If enough of them continue Adah Maurer's work, it will at last be possible to stop the beating of schoolchildren anywhere in the United States once and for all.

A long time ago, a chief of the Nez Percé Indians and a number of his warriors were riding through a United States Army camp on the way to a scheduled peace meeting with American army officers. The chief, passing by an American soldier beating a child, stopped his procession.

Signaling the Indians with him to turn around and leave the camp, the chief of the Nez Percé said, "There is no way to talk about peace to barbarians. What could you say to anyone who would strike a child?"

A few years ago, Adah Maurer received a letter from a West German who had seen a copy of her newsletter, *The Last ?*

Resort, and was astonished to find that children were still being
officially beaten in American schools.

He told Adah Maurer, "After the war, Americans forced
Germany to abolish corporal punishment in [German] schools.
We were no longer allowed to conduct our schools in an au-
thoritarian manner.

"Now I discover that the Americans, all the time they
were making rules for us about not using corporal punishment,
were themselves doing it and still continue to do so!"

VI

WHEN
THE BILL OF RIGHTS
COMES INTO
YOUR LIFE

14

Supreme Court Justice William Brennan is a passionate defender of individual liberties and rights. As we saw in the case of Diane Doe—the young student from Indiana who was subject to a search by police dogs and then a strip-search by police —Justice Brennan is as concerned about the rights of the young as he is about the rights of adults.

In 1985, when the majority of the Supreme Court (in *New Jersey* v. *T.L.O.*) said for the first time that public school students do have Fourth Amendment (privacy) rights, Brennan agreed. But when the same majority, in the same case, greatly weakened those rights by saying that students could be searched in school under a lower standard than adults can be searched in or out of schools, Brennan vigorously dissented.

Because of the *New Jersey* v. *T.L.O.* decision, school principals and teachers can now search students even if they do not have "probable cause" for that search. "Probable cause" is the standard that police use for searching adults; it means that those making the search must first know of facts that would lead a prudent person to believe that a specific crime has been committed, or that specific evidence relating to a crime is at a specific place, such as in a locker or in a purse.

But a majority of the Supreme Court decided in *T.L.O.* that where students are concerned, all the school authorities need are "reasonable grounds" on which to base a search. That's a much looser, vaguer standard than "probable cause."

In his dissent, Justice Brennan, insisting that the "probable cause" standard should apply to students, pointed out that
the Fourth Amendment's protections of "personal privacy and
personal security" are of special importance in schools. Young
people, he emphasized, learn as much by example as by what
they're told in books. So if students see a teacher or principal
acting in a way that is disrespectful of the students' right to
privacy, they're not going to believe that the Constitution has
much of anything to do with them.

Even the majority of the Supreme Court in the *T.L.O.* decision did not say, it should be pointed out, that general searches
(in which a whole class or school are targeted) are Constitutional. The "reasonable grounds" for a search must apply to
individual students, and no search can be "excessively intrusive." And although teachers and administrators do not have to
go by the higher standard of "probable cause," policemen
called in to a school still must use that higher standard—and
they must have a warrant, unless it's an emergency.

Some years ago, Justice Brennan had something else to say
about what happens in schoolrooms. As noted earlier in this
book, he said he was greatly troubled "that so many Americans
fail to understand the deeper meaning of our Bill of Rights. I
do not suggest that students cannot recite the text of the first
ten amendments—on the whole that seems to be done quite
smoothly. What does concern me deeply is that *the impact of the
words of the Bill of Rights very often fails to get off the printed page
and into real life.* (Emphasis added.)

On a crisp October day in 1981, I had a chance to see what
can happen when the Bill of Rights does get off the printed
page and becomes real to students.

I was in Kanawha County, West Virginia, where in 1974 a
large number of parents had become furious at the presence of
certain textbooks in the public schools. In their view, these
books were subversive of religious, family, and patriotic values.
Their indignant protests led to, among other things, shotgun

blasts shattering windows in the board of education building in Charleston. Eventually, the building itself was shut down for a time.

The war of the textbooks also resulted in four thousand miners going out on strike in solidarity with the protesting parents. (Eventually, the textbooks stayed in the schools, but officials decided that two of the series of books could be used only for supplemental reading, and then only with parental consent.)

It was on that rough battlefield of Kanawha County that the West Virginia affiliate of the American Civil Liberties Union and several other libertarians decided to hold a Bill of Rights Day in Charleston for high school seniors—beginning early in the morning and lasting until evening. It had taken about a year to get permission from the school board for the release of the students, who were to assemble in a spacious local church. I was told that members of the school board had been apprehensive. They were worried that news of the exposure of so many students to some of the ideas in the Bill of Rights might bring out the shotguns again.

For a week before that Bill of Rights Day in 1974, the high school seniors had been assigned readings and had engaged in class discussion of freedom of speech and press, the separation of church and state, cruel and unusual punishment, the occasional difficulties of having a free press and a fair trial at the same time, and other dilemmas of liberty.

On the day itself, the youngsters came, one hundred fifty of them, from the city of Charleston and from the "hollers," the valleys within the steep hills outside the city. The students were separated into twelve groups. In each, they were given both actual case histories and hypothetical cases. In exploring some of the cases, the students acted out roles in the Constitutional dramas.

During the course of the day, for instance, certain students became cops confronted by deliberately provocative demon-

strators advocating—but not engaging in—violence. Others became parents insisting that certain books must be removed
from the schools because they were plainly obscene, unpatri-
otic, and blasphemous. Still other students turned into librarians trying to point out that if library books and textbooks were
purchased according to the majority vote of the community,
only the least controversial books would survive, and the students would grow up vastly ignorant in many subject areas.

In the group I was working with, the dialogues were intense, not only during the working out of the cases but also
during the breaks in the discussion. And I saw much the same
crackling intellectual and emotional energy in the other groups
scattered around the church.

By early evening, I was through, the students in my group
having put all remaining questions to a vote to see if anyone
had turned around over the hours. Most had on one issue or
another. Other units around the church were still trying to
make sense out of the Constitution and each other.

I walked over to one of the groups. The students there
were being told by a teacher leading the discussion that a
bunch of West Virginians, members of a Communist splinter
group, had decided to march up and down the streets of
Charleston, brandishing red flags. They were also going to
carry inflammatory, insulting signs denouncing the President,
the Constitution, and calling for the overthrow of the government.

The question: Do these Communists, even under the First
Amendment, have the right to so grievously offend decent
folks, including innocent children, on the streets of Charleston?
And since they are calling for the overthrow of the government, was the Constitution intended to be a suicide pact? Was it
intended to give sworn enemies of our liberty the freedom to
try to gain converts who would destroy that liberty?

Furthermore, if the march were allowed, some of these
Communists—as had actually happened during an aborted

demonstration by the Communist Workers Party in Charleston a year before—would surely be beaten up. With the high probability of violence, including likely violence to innocent bystanders, isn't it more vital to protect the public peace by forbidding the march than to allow the demonstration?

The students argued loudly. I was particularly watching a slight young woman with thin brown hair, maybe seventeen, who had said very little all day long and had not yet said a word during this discussion. As she listened, she was biting her lip. Suddenly, in a soft voice—which somehow silenced all the others—she started speaking very slowly, more to herself than to the rest of us.

"Well," she said, rubbing her nose, "I was there last year when they beat up those Communists. I didn't think much about it one way or the other." She bit her lip again. "If I had, I guess I would have done some beating up myself. But now"—she screwed up her face—"well, after all I've been hearing and thinking today, well, maybe they do have a right to go out there and march."

She paused, and said even more slowly, "And I guess they got a right not to get beat up doing it, no matter what they say, no matter how awful their signs are." She shook her head. "It's hard. But I guess I don't see no other way."

The young woman slipped into the background as another senior, shaking his head vigorously in disagreement, said, "No, I don't see that at all. Communists have no rights. They want to take away *our* rights. It's just plain stupid to let them go around doing that. What I say is let them go back where they came from."

"But they're all West Virginians, remember?" said the teacher leading the discussion.

The young man thought about it for a few seconds, and said, "Well, let's kick them out of West Virginia. Send them to New York or Russia or some place like that."

The debate became more heated until finally there was a

vote, and a majority of the unit sided with the hard conclusion of the shy young woman, who had not said another word.

I was standing next to a woman who lived in Charleston and had helped organize this Bill of Rights Day. "You see," she said, "if you just give them a chance to think about these things and work them out inside their heads, the Bill of Rights gets right off the page and comes alive. Why doesn't this sort of thing happen more often around the country?"

I think of that day in Kanawha County often. I expect that some of the students there have not forgotten it either.

In addition to the basics—learning how to read, write and *think*—there is no more important work to be done in schools than to make freedom *personal*. Freedom of speech and press, freedom of religion, freedom from government violations of privacy—all the liberties that must come off the printed page and into real life if this nation is to remain free.

The people in this book are among the contemporary Americans who have put themselves at risk to keep the Bill of Rights as vital a part of real life as the Framers of the Constitution intended. They all have learned, in different ways, what the shy high school senior in Charleston, West Virginia, found out: liberty is indivisible. If it doesn't belong to everyone, even people you despise, it isn't secure for anyone. Including you.

And in nations where liberty is not as natural as the rhythms of the air and of the sea, creativity of all kinds—in the arts, in the sciences, in daily life—withers away, as in the Soviet Union, Chile, Cuba, South Africa. What is left in such countries are the "official" arts, the "official" sciences, and officially supervised lives, all of them drained of individuality, unpredictability, and dignity.

One last thing: each of you, living in a country that was created in a revolution for freedom, have many satisfactions ahead as you discover how to be your own person under the Constitution.

You may lose some battles on behalf of the Bill of Rights, and you'll win some. Whatever happens, so long as you care about your own liberties and those of others, you will be able to look in the mirror and keep seeing a real live free American.

FURTHER READING

Brant, Irving. *The Bill of Rights*. New York: Mentor, New American Library, 1967.

Downs, Robert B., and Ralph E. McCoy, eds. *The First Freedom Today: Critical Issues Relating to Censorship and to Intellectual Freedom*. Chicago: American Library Association, 1984.

Epstein, Sam, and Beryl Epstein. *Kids in Court: The ACLU Defends Their Rights*. New York: Four Winds Press, 1982.

Hentoff, Nat. *The First Freedom: The Tumultuous History of Free Speech in America*. New York: Dell, 1981.

Levy, Leonard W. *Emergence of a Free Press*. New York: Oxford University Press, 1985.

Mee, Charles L., Jr. *The Genius of the People*. New York: Harper & Row, 1987.

Peters, William. *A More Perfect Union: The Making of the United States Constitution*. New York: Crown Publishers, 1987.

Zerman, Melvyn Bernard. *Taking on the Press: Constitutional Rights in Conflict*. New York: Thomas Y. Crowell, 1986.

ABOUT THE AUTHOR

NAT HENTOFF, nationally acclaimed for his writing on civil liberties and jazz, was born in Boston, Massachusetts. A graduate of Northeastern University, he did graduate work at Harvard and studied at the Sorbonne on a Fulbright fellowship. He is now a staff writer for *The Village Voice* and *The New Yorker*, a columnist for *The Washington Post*, and contributes regularly to various national publications.

Nat Hentoff's most recent book for Delacorte Press was *The Day They Came to Arrest the Book*, which followed *Does This School Have Capital Punishment?* and *This School Is Driving Me Crazy* (all available in Dell Laurel-Leaf editions). He is also the author of *The First Freedom: The Tumultuous History of Free Speech in America*, available in Delacorte and Dell Laurel editions. His autobiography, *Boston Boy*, was recently published as well.

The father of four children, Nat Hentoff lives in New York City.

INDEX